There's a Hamster in the Dashboard

Also by David W. Berner

Accidental Lessons
After Opium: Stories
Knowing What to Steal
Any Road Will Take You There

There's a Hamster in the Dashboard

A Life in Pets

David W. Berner

There's a Hamster in the Dashboard: A Life in Pets

First Dream of Things edition, 2015
Published by Dream of Things, Downers Grove, Illinois USA
dreamofthings.com

Dream of Things provides discounts to educators, book clubs, writers groups, and others. Contact customerservice@ dreamofthings.com or call 847-321-1390.

Publisher's Cataloging-in-Publication data:
Berner, David W.
    There's a hamster in the dashboard : a life in pets / David W. Berner.
    p. cm.
    ISBN 978-0-9908407-1-8

1. Berner, David W. 2. Pets. 3. Animals --Anecdotes. 4. Parenting.
I. Title.

SF416 .B47 2015
636 --dc23   2015938878

Book design: Susan Veach

Contents

For Gloria

Acknowledgements

I am eternally grateful to all of those who encouraged me to write this book, and to those who read many of the early drafts, offered comments and ideas, and prodded me along when the stories were stuck in the mud.

This book would not exist without my friend, editor, and publisher Mike O'Mary. His keen eye and insight were of immeasurable importance.

The fuel that powered me through the writing came from the care and kindness of many people, most notably Leslie O'Hare. Without her loving encouragement, the manuscript might have been far too ragged to permit anyone to see it.

The soul of this book belongs to those who shared with me the remarkable experiences of these stories—my mother, Gloria; my father, Norman; my sister, Diane; Marie Berner; my paternal and maternal grandmothers; my aunt Jackie Woods; old friends and neighbors from the streets where I grew up; my boyhood town's police officers; my elementary school teachers; all those pet store clerks; and most important, my two sons Casey and Graham, for they are the lanterns of my life.

"Love the animals.
God has given them the rudiments of thought and joy untroubled."
— Fyodor Dostoyevsky

Preface

There's a moment in the early morning, just before the sun rises, when my yellow lab arrives at the side of my bed, rests her nose on the mattress, nuzzles her snout into the sheets, and wags her tail so vigorously it wildly collides with everything in its way. Rhythmic thumps strike the wall and reverberate throughout the house. She's knocked books off the nightstand and once whacked a table lamp to the floor. And every time, she is completely unaware of how this exuberant flailing is a rather discourteous wake-up call. To her it is simply a joyful "good morning," an involuntary signal of how happy she is to be alive, ready for a walk, and to be with me.

Pets are so pure. They are undeniably honest, so utterly real. And every morning, with the beating of that tail, I am reminded of this.

My dog and all the pets that came before her have shown unwavering love. And with every one, I've tried my best to show it back. I've gone on hundreds of walks, thrown dozens of Frisbees and tennis balls, and given in to sad-eyed puppies whining to be allowed into my bed. I've picked up truckloads of dog poop, mopped up canine throw-up, and cleaned filthy litter boxes. I've held dying dogs in my arms, helped bury cats, and even organized a funeral for a hamster. I've scraped out the muck in fish bowls, watched ants escape from an ant farm, and carried a turtle home in a golf bag. And all of it—the good, the bad, and the misguided—was absolutely worth it, even if I might not have believed it at the time.

But there were moments when I should have known better.

It's not as if someone forced me to own a pet. I accepted, purchased, or adopted each one with complete free will. I never entered a relationship with a pet at gunpoint. And, I don't believe I've been an inadequate, inept pet owner, although I could have done better in what now seem to be achingly obvious cases. The thing is, I've been fascinated by animals, all kinds, always have. But as with caring for children, I could have used some guidance—and I think that's probably true for anybody who has cared for a pet or raised a child.

As mothers and fathers, we all have our anxieties, doubts about this most important job. We attempt to do the very best we can. We read instruction books from the so-called experts. We ask lots of questions. We make regular appointments with doctors and dentists. We escort our children to school, play groups, and soccer practice. But sometimes, even with the best of intentions, we screw up. We should have thought something through, tried harder, been more attentive, more responsive. It's not that we don't love them—our kids or our pets—it's just that we are helplessly human.

Each of the stories in this collection touches on an accidental revelation or challenging moment that could only have been experienced while being an ordinary and not-so-ordinary pet owner, probably just like many of you. Yes, like you, I've tried—

sometimes not very well—to care for a bevy of creatures and through that process have learned plenty, more than I could have imagined. Not in some formal educational way like the lecture of a professor or the homily of a preacher, but more like an unexpected gradual awakening, like the sun burning through fog. You don't even know it's there until it's warming you and lighting the way. But most important, I've experienced that beautifully simple yet immensely profound instant when a pet owner connects, almost spiritually, with an animal in an unparalleled bond of man and beast—clear evidence that the creature you've allowed into our life is really an extension of yourself. That's what these stories are all about—those magnificent relationships, the love of family, and the uniqueness of each existence shared with the living and breathing. These are the personal stories of a life with pets, those remarkable companions that allow us to catch ourselves being human.

The Intelligence of Dogs

There have been a number of times when I have seriously questioned if my pets had any brains at all. Dogs, at least certain breeds, are said to be pretty bright creatures. But why does my Labrador retriever try to eat her own feces? Then there was the family wheaten terrier, which never quite understood the car thing, repeatedly busting out of the backyard and running out into the middle of the street even after a Toyota Camry clipped his hind end once. You think he would have figured it out.

There are numerous lists out there on the smartest dogs, each compiled by veterinarians or dog whispers or animal behaviorists. Border collies are at the top of most of these lists. Poodles and German shepherds rank high. Labs are in the upper ten. Wheaten terriers, like Hogan, show up around forty. My father used to joke about Hogan's lack of smarts. "Dust," he'd say, his hands placed on either side of Hogan's head. "Dust. Nothing but dust." According to the experts, he may have been right.

Despite this, most dog owners will insist their pet has some uncanny sensitivity. The dog feels thunderstorms coming on, or senses a ghost in the house, or knows when its master is coming home even before the door opens. I don't know if that's about intelligence or about some sixth sense or innate behavior. Maybe it's simply biological, the heightened senses of canines—smell or hearing. But it's something we as humans always find intriguing, even astonishing. Animal magic. And this was very much the case with my boyhood dog, Sally.

My grandfather gave me the collie on my first birthday, so the dog became part of my every step growing up. And one incident in particular confirmed that Sally was far more than just a boy's dog.

I was three years old. My mother turned her head for just a moment, she said, and I was off on an adventure. I slipped out the front door and toddled my way down the steep street in front of our home. Naked. Absolutely bare-bottomed.

Now, there's a lot you can say, if you want to, about how this kind of thing could have possibly happened. You could condemn my mother for not watching me more carefully. You could question her parenting skills. But the truth was that my getaway was quite innocent. It was summer, we had no air conditioning, and so a kid running around naked was not at all odd. The windows were open, and the front door probably was unlocked—as it always was in our quiet neighborhood in a leafy suburb of Pittsburgh. And, I've been told, I absolutely loved being outside when I was little. All this presented the perfect storm for a daring little boy.

I don't recall all the details of this incident—I was so young then—but I'm told I walked down the driveway to the street and then made a right turn down the hill toward where my grandmother lived, about seven houses away. I was right in the middle of the road, just waddling along with great purpose, as if I was undeniably, one hundred percent supposed to be there.

About halfway down the street, a neighbor spotted me from her kitchen window.

"Do you know where your son is?" This is how my mother remembered the neighbor's words in a phone call to our house. "He's happy as ever; just out for a stroll. But he also looks like he's on a mission, like he knows exactly where he's going. Oh, and now," said the neighbor, pausing momentarily, "the dog's there, too."

Sally came sprinting from behind. When she caught up, she started to bark and then nudge her nose on my butt and belly.

"The dog is dancing around him like she wants to play or something," the neighbor told my mother.

The neighbor was at first startled seeing me alone and naked. She told my mother she felt awful it took her several minutes just to consider telephoning our house.

Sally kept barking, nudging. I kept walking. Then Sally started to run in a circle around me as I traveled, spinning as if she were herding sheep.

Mom hung up the phone, dropped the laundry basket she'd been carrying, and hurried out the door.

By this time I was all the way down the street, but I was no longer walking away from home. I was now walking back. Sally, with her persistent shepherding, had turned me around, poking my behind with her snout and pointing me homeward.

My mother was part of the way down the block when she stopped and instead of frantically chasing after me, she simply watched. There was Sally, edging me up the hill. Then, spotting my mother, Sally began to bark again. My mother said she didn't know whether to be angry, grateful, or astounded.

"I knew Sally was a good dog," she said. "But I had never seen a dog do anything like that."

Mom grabbed my arm and gave me a slap on the butt—just enough to get my attention—and then crouched down, wrapped me in her arms, and pulled me in tight. Sally began to whimper and lick my face. My mother hugged her, looked Sally in the eyes, and softly said, "Thank you, girl."

For years afterward, my mother loved telling this story, and she'd offer it to anyone who would listen. "It was like a scene from *Lassie*, the old television show," she'd say. Some doubted the story, but my mother always insisted she knew what she saw—and she saw a dog rescue her wayward son. "Why would anyone make that up?" she would wonder aloud.

My mother always believed there was some higher power, some mystic force in the world that guided us. She was brought up Catholic, and although she was never bound by the dogma, she was certain there was some supernatural link between living things. Mom not only talked to her pets, she talked to the rhododendron bush in her garden, and swore her words were the reason it blossomed to perfection every spring.

For the next nine years of Sally's life, she and I were inseparable. She followed me when I played baseball with my friends in the grave-less section of the old cemetery on the other side of the woods. She'd sit quietly beside the shallow plastic wading pool in our backyard and watch as I splashed and pretended to be Lloyd Bridges, the star of TV's *Sea Hunt*. I threw soft snowballs at her and laughed as they exploded in her mouth when she tried to catch them. She slept in my bed.

I still don't know whether it was simply instinct or intelligence, but I like to think what Sally did that summer afternoon when I was a little boy was the work of a super smart, super aware, highly attuned dog motivated by love.

The Secret Lives of Ants

I t was on the second-to-last page of a Batman comic book, or maybe it was *Mad* magazine. Either way, it was right next to the advertisements for sea monkeys, a set of Civil War soldiers, and X-ray glasses. And it was what I and a lot of my friends wanted. It was not as if they were the ultimate, coolest pets of all time or anything close to that. In fact, anyone could find them in the cracks of the sidewalk right outside your house. Drop a little candy on the ground, and they'd be all over it—hundreds of them. But what was cool, way cool, was the home you kept them in. Uncle Milton's Ant Farm looked like the most amazing thing ever, and it made me want to spend every last penny of my allowance money to get one.

The soldiers had a different appeal, and the possible purpose of X-ray glasses wasn't yet clear to a seven-year old. The sea monkeys unquestionably looked exotic, but if you answered the ad and ordered the sea creatures, then you'd have to buy other things—the entire habitat and lots of other paraphernalia. Uncle Milton's Ant Farm had all a kid needed, everything in one kit—the rectangular, narrow, plastic, see-through habitat; a bag of sandy soil; and a vial of ants.

I saved up $2.98, plus a few cents for handling, and ordered my very own.

Milton Levine was an interesting guy. His story was framed around the American Dream and powered by entrepreneurial gusto. When Milt returned to his Pittsburgh home from military duty overseas in 1946, he and his brother-in-law saw the opportunity only the coming baby boom could deliver. They started a mail order business. It was all about novelties, and their first product included animal balloons and plastic shrunken heads, like something from a secret primitive South American tribe. They moved on to dwarf trees and then army soldiers and sea monkeys. Yep, the "100 soldiers for $1" was Milt's. And those sea monkeys? Also Milt. For about ten years, Milt and his brother-in-law churned out this stuff. Then in 1956, as the story goes, Milt was at a picnic and saw ants on the ground. He recalled how the insects would always fascinate his kids, how they'd watch them scurry around, observing for hours how the ants would carry crumbs to their little dirt hills and underground homes. Bingo. Uncle Milton's Ant Farm was born.

It wasn't really a farm, per se. You didn't "raise" ants. It was actually a formicarium, a habitat that allowed you to study ants. The little plastic unit had a glass-like window pane where you could watch the industrious insects work their little ant antennae off. They built these intricate tunnels through the sandy dirt. Drop seeds in the farm to feed them, and they stored them in cave-like compartments. And when one of their own died, these worker ants carried the body to the place where dead ants go, a kind of graveyard or mausoleum deep in the channels. It appeared to be done with great care, even reverence. It was a secret subterranean world and watching it was like spying; it had a Peeping Tom element to it and it captivated me. I was getting a peek inside a world that had, until then, literally gone underground. This was plenty of adventure for me. The lusty temptation of the X-ray glasses and the secrets they might reveal hadn't occurred yet to this pre-pubescent. I hadn't considered how my allowance money might have been better spent on science fiction spectacles so I could find out what was under the dress of the blonde in the second row of my English class. That would come later, of course, only to find those glasses didn't work a lick. But I kind of knew that would be the case. So, before the hormones kicked in, the ant farm was my best chance to uncover mysteries.

Maybe I'm overstating this, but it's possible that the ant farm and my early fascination with it fueled my first desire to dig deeper into things. I've worked as a journalist, a writer, and a teacher for many years, and that is what one does in those professions, right? Unearth things? We expose. We dig up facts. Discover things. We excavate human emotions. And all of this is based in the wonderfully vibrant motivation of curiosity. Plus— and here is where I may be really stretching it—maybe the ant farm began to open up my young boy's mind and move it away from its propensity for prejudice.

I wasn't a huge fan of bugs as a kid. Like most boys, I had a healthy youngster's interest in the creepy, but I wasn't in any way an insect nut. Not like Mark, the boy next door who collected moths and centipedes. What did I know about ants? What did I care about them, really? I saw friends light matches and burn them for fun. I saw kids step on them, kill them without a single thought or any remorse. In fact, they did it with glee. If you found one crawling on your leg, you'd slap it dead, flick it off with a finger, and never think twice. But once I got to know ants—once I witnessed up close their lives, their work, their sense of community and home—it changed me. It must have.

Or maybe I'm full of crap. Maybe Uncle Milton's Ant Farm was just a simple diversion, slightly better at times than Bugs Bunny cartoons on Saturday morning. Sometimes though, when we are paying the least attention, we are shaped into who we are. Isn't that true? The molding comes subtly, the work of crafty Karma. It's simplistic, but true: we become who we are by where we've been, who we've been with, by all that has surrounded us, all that we have permitted into our daily existence. It may come in a flash or it may work to shape us in a more methodical, stealth-like way, tiptoeing into our reality undetected.

I had Uncle Milton's Ant Farm for a long time—maybe six months or so, an eternity for a kid. And I would have kept it even longer if I could have. But I dropped it on the concrete side porch of our home, and unknowingly cracked the plastic. It was just enough to allow the ants to later squeeze out, so I had to get rid of Uncle Milt's invention. Mom found ants crawling all over my dresser, the floor, and even my bed. She had to step on some, crush others with bathroom tissue, and finally was forced to spray my entire bedroom with Raid. Still, I'm certain some managed to escape.

Looking back at the ant farm now as an adult, it seemed a bit cruel, the ants locked inside that plastic home. Sure, it gave a young boy a window into a fascinating world he otherwise would never have known and gave me some tiny insight into the life of those industrious insects. But what I really took from those days with the ant farm had nothing to do with how I managed their captivity. Instead, what I remember most is their unexpected freedom. Sometimes now whenever I feel trapped or confined by work, overcome by responsibilities, or buried with grown-up stuff, I think of those ants and how they finally got away.

And Then There Was This Cat

We had four cats when I was a kid. Not at the same time, but over the years. Maybe there were five…I don't exactly recall. But the number of cats really isn't the point.

I have to admit the cats didn't leave the same kind of impression on me as the dogs. It's not that I didn't like the felines. I did. But I've always been more of a dog guy. You know how that goes. People are cataloged as dog or cat people, some ardently on one side or the other. I was a little less zealous about it. But despite my allegiance to dogs, there was this one cat that was impossible to forget.

My father named it.

"Mouse," he said with conviction. "Let's call it something that no one has ever called a cat before."

The name was funny at the time. My little sister and I were somewhere around ages four and ten, and I'm certain that's partly why the silly name seemed so amusing. Still, that was the cat's name, and there's no question this feline lived up to its quirky label.

The cat didn't act like a mouse, no rodent characteristics. The name Mouse was chosen because it was just so *out there*. My father—the kind of guy who had the same Saturday tee time at the local golf course for years and climbed into the same stained white painter's pants every evening after work for months before washing them—was a man of routine and suburban steadiness. But every once in a while he liked doing the unexpected. And what was more unexpected than to name a cat after the predator's prey?

The cat looked like a lot of others: black with white paws and another white blotch under its neck. There also was a thin strip of white on its head that led down to its nose. It also had this glare, a real intense stare, a curious, bewildering devilment, as if schemes were being hatched behind its misty, green eyes. And at times those eyes appeared maniacal. They would change, become twitchy, the lids shutting ever so slightly as if Mouse was squinting, peering at something no one else could see. And then, he would go nuts. My father called these episodes "Mouse fits." The cat unexpectedly would begin to spin on the carpeted floor, as if chasing its tail, becoming a blur. Then it would stop suddenly, as if screeching on the brakes, look at us for just a split second, then dart behind the couch. You'd hear frantic scratching, and then Mouse's head would pop up from behind the back of the couch, like a jack-in-the-box, just enough to see its ears, top of the head, and those freaky eyes. Then, just as quickly, Mouse would vanish. There'd be more agitated scratching from under the couch, and then a dash across the living room, through the kitchen, into the dining room, and up the stairs. You could hear his frenzied pace across the ceiling as he bolted around the bedrooms. Mouse would then zip back downstairs, do that spin move again on the floor, stop suddenly and, like a kid's toy when the batteries run out, he'd abruptly stop. Mouse would then roll slowly on his back. Lastly, as if possessed by an entirely different motivation, he'd stroll nonchalantly to the chair next to the fireplace, crawl almost elegantly to the top of the seat's back, gracefully leap to the mantel, softly curl into a ball, delicately dangle a leg over the edge, and fall asleep.

"Really? That's what he does?" This was the response from our vet when we told him about those "Mouse fits."

"What could be going on here?" my mother asked.

"I have no earthly idea," the vet said, smiling. "Crazy cat."

Yep. Crazy cat.

In many ways, Mouse was more like a dog than a cat. He would come when you'd call his name, he'd lie at your feet when you'd sit at the dinner table, go for car rides, follow me around like a puppy when I'd play in the backyard. He learned to do his business outside and not in a litter box, and he even shunned regular cat food, opting to eat Purina from our dog's bowl. We had the dog first, and maybe Mouse simply learned this peculiar eating habit from observation. "Don't think so," the vet responded when we asked if that was possible. "Cat's don't imitate. They do what they want." Maybe Mouse simply wanted to be a dog.

I don't remember how long we had Mouse or how old he was when he left. Mouse got sick. He was losing weight and becoming sluggish. The "Mouse fits" happened less frequently. I'm sure we took him to the vet, but I don't remember the diagnosis or what the vet may have suggested. I just remember waking up one morning and finding my mother in the kitchen, wiping away tears. "I think Mouse has left to go to heaven," she said. Mouse was an outside cat, pretty common in the neighborhood when I was a kid, and when we let him out at night, he would always return in the early morning for breakfast. But one morning he didn't, and my mother just knew that Mouse was not coming back. Dad held out hope. He thought maybe Mouse would eventually return. But Mouse never did. This was one of the first real windows into the true emotional life of my mother and father, outside of the love they showed toward me. I saw my mother's compassion, her wide capacity for unconditional love. But maybe more important, I saw the first inklings of what I would come to know as my father's utterly positive view on life. He was a baby of the Great Depression, a man of a generation of men who disguised emotions and lived in a definitive wrong-and-right, back-and-white world. He could be brusque, impatient, and matter-of-fact, but with matters of the heart my father was a softy. He camouflaged it well, but there were times when he would permit faith and optimism to prevail, allowing each to peek out from behind a heavy curtain.

A few months after Mouse was gone, we got another cat. My father named it Tom, a clichéd name, really. It seemed Dad wanted a name that was nothing like Mouse, nothing like that extraordinarily odd and wonderful cat.

A Gerbil Wedding

There's a certain kind of pet you could call a "starter pet." These are the ones that test you, the ones your parents agree to buy to see if you might show some level of responsibility. And maybe, just maybe, if you do well, they'll allow you to graduate to a cat or a dog, a real pet.

My starter pet was Tony the gerbil.

Tony wasn't really a starter, per se. Our family already had a dog when we got Tony from the local pet store. But it still was the kind of pet that could prompt a young boy to start thinking about the well-being of another living thing, especially since I would be held accountable for its care. My parents did all the work with our dog, not me. I was just a baby when the collie came into our home, so I really didn't have dog duties. The dog may have been the family pet, but the gerbil was all mine.

"It'll be up to you, David," my mother warned. "And if you can't take care of it, we'll have to give it to someone who can." It was a mild threat. My mother wasn't very good with threats.

I was a first grader and a gerbil seemed a very cool idea.

"I can do it, Mom," I said emphatically.

Mom drove our avocado green Chevy Impala to the pet store.

David W. Berner

There were several gerbils in a cage, and I don't remember why I chose the one I did. I just pointed and said, "That one." It was that simple. "Can I call it Tony?" We got some gerbil food in a small box, and, of course, a cage.

"You'll want one with the wheel inside," the pet store clerk said. "A gerbil should get some exercise."

The wheel looked like a ride at a miniature carnival, a tiny little Ferris wheel without the seats. The cage at the pet store was big enough to hold several wheels, and the gerbils seemed to love them. In the twenty minutes or so we spent at the store, there was always a gerbil on a wheel incessantly running to or from absolutely nothing.

We bought cedar shavings to line the bed of the cage.

"Cedar's good. It keeps the smell down," said the clerk.

"Perfect," my mother said.

It never occurred to me that gerbils poop in their cages. I never thought about that little fact, but I would learn soon enough, discovering I'd have to scrub out the cage and put new cedar chips inside every couple of days.

We also bought a water dispenser, a bottle with a spout on it. It hung on the outside of the cage with the dispenser's end slipping inside so Tony could get a sip whenever he wanted.

"Be sure you keep the water full all the time," the clerk warned. "He'll drink a lot."

It was only then that my mother thought about the sex of the gerbil.

"You say *he*. How do you know that?" she asked.

The clerk was puzzled and shrugged her shoulders. "I don't," the clerk said. "I have no idea how to tell if it's a boy or girl."

I had already picked out the name and wasn't about to change it. Tony was the name of my friend who lived up the street. Tony and I were good buds. We watched cartoons together, and on rainy days we played cowboys and Indians on the big front porch of his home, building a pretend fort with the plastic furniture and the milk box. And a couple times during the summer, my mother invited Tony to come to the community pool with us. We splashed in the sun for hours. Tony and I were inseparable. That is, until he moved. Tony left the neighborhood when his father lost his job. I was crushed and cried for a day.

"What if he's a girl?" I asked my mother. "I really want the name to be Tony."

"I don't think it matters much," she said, smiling. "If you want to name it Tony, go right ahead." She patted me on the head and kissed my forehead. She knew how I felt about my friend.

Tony the gerbil was great. He loved his wheel and he gobbled up the food we got him. He'd let me hold him in my lap when I watched *The Flintstones*, his little nose wiggling so fast it appeared to be vibrating. I wanted to believe that Tony was happy. I liked him, and he liked me, I thought. We were buds. And for a little guy just learning the ropes of pet care, I was pretty good at it. I cleaned the cage when I was supposed to, although I didn't like smelling the poop or scooping it out. And there was the smell of urine that I wasn't expecting. Still, I did it. And I liked how it felt when the cage was clean again with new cedar on the bottom and I'd place Tony back inside, giving my gerbil a fresh new home.

After a few months, I wondered if Tony was lonely when I wasn't around.

"I think Tony needs a friend," I said to my mother.

David W. Berner

"He's got you, doesn't he?" she asked.

"I mean, another gerbil friend. I'll bet he misses the ones from the pet store."

I remember my mother's silence. It seemed like forever before she spoke. "Well, maybe you're right."

We went back to the pet store and bought another gerbil. I called it Sam.

The two got along wonderfully. They took turns on the wheel and never fought over the food. They even slept together in the far corner of the cage, snuggling so close they appeared to be one big gerbil. And I still did pretty well with caring for them, even getting both of them to sit in my lap when I was watching TV. Sam and Tony were perfect for each other, and for me. We were all best buds.

One Saturday morning I came down the stairs from my bedroom for breakfast, and as I always did, walked by the cage to say hello to Tony and Sam, give them fresh food, and make sure the water container was full. But this time when I peered inside the cage, things were very different.

"Mom, there are funny pink bubbles in there," I said, bewildered.

My mother looked inside and gasped. "Oh my," she said.

"What it is?" I asked, worried by her reaction.

"Oh my," she said again.

"Mom?" I started to whimper.

"Oh honey, it's okay," Mom said, putting her arms around me. She began to giggle. "I think Sam and Tony got married."

"Married?"

"Those bubbles are babies, sweetie."

Tony was sleeping next to the tiny pink "bubbles," and Sam was on the other side of the cage, sleeping by himself. This was apparently what gerbils do when they give birth. The mother hovers over the babies to protect them from the father. Males will sometimes eat the newborns. Don't know if that's actually true, but it's what the clerk at the pet store told my mother when she telephoned the shop that morning.

"The pet store says we have to get Sam out of the cage," Mom advised.

"What about Tony?" I asked, anxious for an answer.

"Tony, honey," she said, pausing for a moment, "is a Tina."

I didn't know what to say. I was old enough to know girls were the ones who had babies, but I wasn't quite inquisitive enough to delve deeper. All I knew was that Tony the gerbil, my best bud, the one named after the friend who moved away, was no longer the Tony I knew. Oh sure, a gerbil is a gerbil. But I had considered Tony to be *Tony*...not *Tina*. Everything changed. It was as if my best friend had left me all over again. Tony wasn't Tony anymore. Tony was Tina...and a mother. She had babies. I didn't really understand the emotion enveloping me, but I knew I didn't like it. It was as if another friend had left me.

We soon gave Sam away to a neighbor's kid and tried to leave Tina alone with her babies. She had developed a bit of an aggressive streak, the mode of a protective mother. We kept the food and water coming and watched the pink bubbles slowly grow. Brown hair emerged on their tiny bodies, and their once tightly shut eyes opened to the world. As they got bigger, Tina began sleeping on the other side of the cage and occasionally got back on the wheel. In time, I had come to accept Tony as

Tina, and had become somewhat fascinated by the relationship between Tina and her six little gerbils. But, just like most kids, after a while the excitement of it all waned, and it wasn't long after the babies starting growing up that I began ducking my duties as a pet owner. Mom had to remind me to feed and water them, and to clean the cage. Plus, there were several gerbils to tend to now and the work was overwhelming. I liked having Tina and her babies around, but I hated having to work at taking care of all of them. Eventually we gave the babies to the pet store. They were happy to have them, and the clerk said they would find them good homes. And Tina? Although I was sad to see her go, she ended up in a good place. One of the teachers at my elementary school just a few blocks away took her in as a class pet. The teacher was happy to have her. And sometimes after school or during recess, I'd slip into her classroom and watch Tina run and run and run on her wheel.

I could no longer talk to or play with my old friend Tony, the boy up the street who left to live somewhere else, and that still made me sad. Tony the boy, like Tony (now Tina) the gerbil, and I had spent many days together, been through so much, we were real pals. But, unlike my boyhood friend, Tina the gerbil was never really going to leave me. Sure, she wasn't in my home anymore, but I still could see her any day at school if I wanted, and I was certain this friend wasn't ever going to climb into a moving van and go far, far away.

Scary Things

There's a spider in the basement."

This is what my mother said to my father on a weeknight just before dinner.

"You have to go down there and take care of it, Norman."

Dad had just come home from work and hadn't yet taken off his sport coat or his hat—a straw fedora he always wore to the office at the insurance agency. There wasn't a moment to put down his briefcase on the chair near the front door.

"A spider?" Dad asked. He was tired and appeared irritated.

"Yes, a big one. Very big," Mom said, raising her hands to depict a creature several inches long.

"Oh come on, Gloria. You're exaggerating. It's just one of those house spiders." It was early fall and insects seemed to be creeping into our house to find a place to hang out. "It's nothing," Dad insisted.

"I don't care. You have to take care of it," Mom demanded.

My mother was not the kind to be frightened by insects. She wasn't fond of the daddy long-leggers that occasionally showed up in our home's damp basement or the water bugs that appeared in the sink from time to time. I'd seen her crush one or two with a paper towel and then throw them away in the garbage, so I knew she could deal with them. And when a field mouse got in the garage once, she was the one who chased it out with a broom. Still, despite past heroics, Mom wanted nothing to do with the spider in the basement.

"I threw a bucket over the top of it," Mom said.

"You did what?" Dad asked, puzzled.

"I was sorting the laundry on the floor," she said. "I picked up some sheets, and there it was. I thought it was one of the kids' rubbery things. I almost reached down to get it."

In the late 1960s, little rubber insects—flies, centipedes, and spiders—were popular toys. You could buy one in penny gumball machines at the grocery store. My sister and I had a bunch of the creepy-crawlies. Sometimes we'd forget to take them out of our pockets, and they'd end up in the laundry pile.

"A bucket over it?" Dad questioned again, this time with a bit of a smirk.

"Norman. Don't. I'm serious."

My father undid his tie and reached in the refrigerator for a bottle of beer. "I'll take care of it after dinner," he said, dismissively.

"No," she said. "Please take care of it now."

"Jesus Christ, Gloria. It's a stupid spider," Dad snapped. He took a swig of the beer and headed down the steps to the basement. "Really, a bucket?" he asked rhetorically as he descended the stairs.

I had been sitting anxiously at the dinner table where white plates, stainless steel knives and forks, and clear drinking glasses had been neatly arranged on plastic placemats. I could smell something sweet and saucy. I guessed it was the scent of Mom's barbequed pork chops simmering in her black skillet. The meal was one of Dad's favorites. My younger sister sat beside me, using crayons to bring dinosaurs to life inside an oversized coloring book. She wasn't paying much attention to what Mom and Dad had been saying. But I was. *A spider*, I thought. *Could it really be that big?*

Mom stood at the top of the steps with a hand on her hip. She smiled at me. "We'll be eating in a moment," she said. Then she turned to the stairs again. "Well?" she asked.

No response from my father.

"Norman?"

Again, a few seconds of silence. Mom stood erect at the doorway and then leaned into the stairwell.

"Jesus!" Dad cried from below. I could hear the metal bucket clink hard against the concrete floor, suggesting it had been thrown down with force.

"Told him," Mom mumbled to herself, moving to the stove to adjust the heat on the pork chops.

"Jesus Christ!" Dad bellowed. There were quick steps on the stairs.

Mom smiled at my sister and me. "Believe me now?" she asked my father as he burst through the doorway to the kitchen.

"That is not some house spider, that's for damn sure," Dad said.

"Scary, isn't it?" Mom asked.

"It's big. Hairy. Huge."

My sister looked up from her coloring book. "What's down there?" she asked.

"Nothing," Dad answered tersely.

There were a lot of scary things going on in our world that autumn. It had been a few years since the assassination of John F. Kennedy, but the horror of it was still hanging heavy in the air. I was in a second grade reading circle when the word came. My teacher cried, little girls cried, we were sent home early, and I remember the spooky, sad silence in the neighborhood. And then it happened to his brother. I learned of Robert Kennedy's murder while standing in line outside McGibney Elementary, preparing to go inside for one of the final days of the school year. It had been only a few weeks since the murder of Martin Luther King, Jr. When our school got word on both of their deaths, just like they did when the president was shot, our teachers, in hushed and halting tones, tried their best to soothe us, insisting everything was going to be okay, the same way they tried to calm us when the school held its weekly safety drills, the ones that forced us under our desks so we'd be safe when the Russians rained atomic bombs on our classroom.

"Can I see the spider?" I asked.

"Where are those encyclopedias?" Dad wondered.

"On the shelf in the kids' room," Mom said.

My father marched upstairs.

Mom dished out supper and sat down to eat. "Dinner's going to get cold," she hollered toward the ceiling. I could hear the floor above creaking as Dad moved above us. "Norman!" Mom shouted.

Dad's feet hit the stairs. "Think I know what it is," he said, moving purposefully from the second floor to the first. One of the large, white-and-blue Encyclopedia Britannica books was open in his hands as he walked into the kitchen. "It's a wolf spider." Dad turned the book toward us to show the photograph and then sat at the table and began to read.

"Wolf spiders are members of the family Ly…Ly…skodia? Or something. Don't know what that word is," Dad said and then continued to read. "It's from the ancient Greek meaning wolf. They are agile hunters with excellent eyesight. Wolf spiders resemble Tarantulas, but are not related."

"Tarantulas?" I asked uneasily.

"They're not tarantulas," Mom assured me.

Dad continued. "Some wolf spiders can be more than two inches long."

"Bigger than that," Mom interrupted.

"Wolf spiders do not build webs," Dad read. "They instead hunt for food, which usually consists of crickets and mealworms."

"How big is it, Dad?" I asked.

"It's big," he said. "Palm of your hand."

"Can I keep it?" I asked.

"No," Mom said firmly.

"Well, it says here they aren't really a threat," Dad said.

"Absolutely not." Mom glared at my father and lifted a forkful of pork to her mouth. "No," she said before feeding herself.

Dad continued to read from the encyclopedia. "Wolf spiders will inject venom if continually provoked."

"Venom? God, no," said Mom. "Norman, please stop reading that."

"Symptoms of their bite are swelling, mild pain, and itching," Dad continued.

"Can we put it in something?" I asked. "A jar?"

Dad placed the book down. "It would be tricky, but probably."

"Nor–man!" Mom said, sounding out the two syllables of my father's name.

My sister continued to color, looking up every few seconds to listen. Her eyes shifted back-and-forth to whoever was speaking and landed finally on me. "Is it going to be your pet?" she asked.

I said nothing and looked only at my father.

"Maybe not a pet, really," he said to my sister. Then looking at me he added, "But maybe we can keep it for awhile."

I smiled.

Mom sighed. "You can't keep it in the house," she pleaded. "If you're going to put it in something, then go ahead, but the jar, or whatever, stays outside. Honestly, I don't think it's a good idea."

"But I can keep it?" I asked, quite aware of the tiny crack in Mom's resolve.

Mom didn't answer. But Dad did. "Let me see what we can do," he said. "That is quite a spider." He turned to my mother and said, "It'll be fine. Really."

After dinner, Dad and I went to the basement with a cleaned-up, oversized mayonnaise jar. At his workshop table, he poked small holes in the metal lid with a screwdriver and scraped off the label with a knife. "There," he said, raising the jar to eye level. "That'll work."

In a quick and trickily timed maneuver, I lifted the metal bucket off the spider, and Dad slapped the open jar over it. Then, with a cotton shirt from the dirty laundry basket, Dad covered the opening and flipped the jar upright. He shook it to force the spider to the bottom and screwed on the lid.

"There you go," he said.

I held the jar in my hand and eyed the spider. It was eerily still, only the ends of its legs quivering.

"How am I going to feed it?" I asked.

Dad, looking momentarily perplexed, cautiously said, "Well. I think we'll have to work on that. Depends on how long you keep it."

"How long?" I asked.

"We'll see," he said, taking the jar from my hands into his. "That is quite a spider."

The next day I took the spider to my school. Most of the boys in my seventh grade class thought it was the coolest thing ever. Some of the girls did, too, but most shied away. I brought along the encyclopedia and read from it during show-and-tell, and even tried answering questions from my classmates and teacher. Where'd you find it? How'd you get it in the jar? Is it a boy or a girl? Does it bite? What does it eat? Will it get bigger? Does it have a name?

I called it Ralph. I don't know why. Sounded like a fun name that wasn't scary. The spider was scary enough, I thought, without a scary name.

Dad brought home a few small live worms from a bait shop near the river. We opened the jar, tossed a couple in, and swiftly put the top back on. At first, Ralph did nothing. But later, when I came back to look, the worms were gone.

About a week after Mom found Ralph in our basement, Dad thought it was best to let him go. "A spider is really not supposed to be a pet," he said. I knew this day would come, and I knew Dad was right. But I still didn't want to let Ralph go.

One night just after dinner, my father and I went to the end of our backyard near the two big maples next to the fence and I slowly unscrewed the jar. I laid it on its side facing away from us and tapped the bottom, hoping to coax Ralph out.

At first, he didn't move. I tapped again and he began to slowly crawl toward the opening in cautious, methodical steps. Dad lifted the bottom of the jar off the ground and delicately shook it. Ralph jumped slightly, crawled more quickly out of the jar, and jumped again. Then, as Ralph touched grass and dirt, his legs fell into an instinctive rhythm, carrying him around one of the trees and into the brush.

"There he goes," Dad said as we both watched Ralph disappear.

After a moment, I said, "You know, Ralph wasn't really all that scary after you got to know him."

Dad smiled, put the lid back on the jar, and said, "No, he wasn't. Not really scary at all."

History has marked the spring, summer, and fall of 1968 as one of the most tumultuous times in America. The ghosts of all those scary events in that singular year still cast enormous, yet ill-defined shadows. To this day I am fascinated with the tenor of those times, the same way I was fascinated with that big spider. And maybe because I lived with that arachnid for awhile—fed it, cared for it, showed it off—I've come to see that a few things, including the aftershocks of violent times, may not be as frightening as they first seem. Even if the fear is truly palpable, you hope you learn to brace yourself and go out into the world anyway.

Three Days with a Squirrel

Think of an animal that you're certain you could never, not in a million years, take on as pet, yet maybe, in some fantasy or dream, would still consider the irrational possibility of making this wild, even exotic creature your own. Sure, there are the reptile lovers, the snake people, and the guy with a Komodo dragon. But they are of a certain kind, a breed of pet owner unto themselves. What I'm really considering here are the rest of us. Think about it. Everyone covets a cute panda bear, right? Then there's the koala, of course. Even a raccoon can look cute. The baby tiger, baby kangaroo, or the baby orangutan that makes an appearance on a late night talk show—the handler widely smiling and proudly showing it off to the host and the audience—can trigger our desires to own one. And why are the stuffed animals at the carnival almost always representations of these loveable wild creatures? Because we know we can't have the real ones, so instead, we awkwardly carry back home an over-sized blue, fluffy, cartoonish, baby elephant.

I wanted a squirrel.

David W. Berner

For some, squirrels are weird, little rodents. But I grew up in the era of *The Secret Squirrel Show*, the star of which was an animated TV character based on the popular spy shows that were all over the television in the mid-60s. This was a very cool squirrel, I'll have you know, a cartoon undercover agent that just happened to be a trench coat wearing, agile, bushy-tailed, tree-dwelling nut eater with an overbite. I think you can still find episodes of *The Secret Squirrel Show* on the Cartoon Network.

But it wasn't solely the television program that had me longing for a squirrel. There were lots of trees in our back and front yards, and squirrels were part of the daily landscape. I'd see them leap across the branches of the massive cherry tree, cling to the tree, and dash to the ground. They'd frantically nibble their nuts and wiggle their noses. To me, they were cute, cuddly, and somehow fascinating in a squirrelly little way.

Consider their quickness. It's uncanny, really. They can turn and zip past you in an instant. They can descend a tree headfirst. Pretty tricky. Try it sometime. And their vision is said to be like magic, detecting seeds or nuts dozens of yards away while still visually spotting danger in the periphery. And even though a squirrel's brain is said to be the size of a walnut at best, there's a lot going on in there. Did you know when you see a squirrel in the road, seemingly erratically darting back and forth as if it doesn't know what to do about your rapidly approaching car, it is actually trying to trick you? Behaviorists claim the squirrel's deceptively unpredictable path in the street is really an attempt to confuse the driver of the car. The squirrel is working to outsmart *you*. Granted, the consequences can be dire for the squirrel, but I like believing that a squirrel has the ability to use some instinctive

36

reasoning, for lack of a better description, as a way to challenge us, even outmaneuver us. Overall, squirrels communicate in a fairly sophisticated way. Those chirps you hear can mean anything from anger to laughter, and animal behaviorists say a squirrel's big tail can say much, gesturing signals to other squirrels. The particular twitch of a female's tail might be a come-on, a way to flirt. And since they mate just once a year, choosing a partner is a picky process. The courting is a series of chases with the female's choice usually determined by the strength of the male squirrel, the stronger and most agile wins the girl. The babies come in litters. They're born naked, toothless, and blind. It takes about eight weeks to grow up and head off on their own.

My squirrel, the one I found struggling on the ground in my backyard, was likely about four weeks old. It was still very much a baby. The vet said he believed its young age and its injury were probably the reasons the squirrel didn't attempt to bite me when I picked it up and put it in a shoebox. It hadn't learned that defensive behavior just yet, he thought. He also scolded me. It was not a good idea to touch a squirrel, any squirrel, let alone pick it up with my bare hands. It could have bitten me and squirrels might carry rabies, he insisted. That, of course, never crossed my mind. I simply saw the squirming squirrel, hurt somehow, and I reacted.

The squirrel's leg was damaged, maybe after being attacked. There was a hawk that hung around in the trees in our yard, diving for rabbits. Maybe its talons ripped into the squirrel, although I'm not sure why the hawk wouldn't have finished off the helpless animal. But how the squirrel received the injury wasn't what interested me. I wanted instead to help it, nurse it back to health. The vet was not about to endorse that idea, and my mother knew he was right. But for some reason she let me give it a try anyway.

I named it Nicky.

Nicky was about the size of a grown man's hand. The eyes were big and brown; they appeared almost too big for its head. And the tail was just beginning to get bushy, although the squirrel's fur was still very much in the growing stage. I put some sticks and leaves in the shoe box, thinking it would somehow feel more like a home, and placed a handful of bird seed in the box's corner for food. The squirrel was so hurt or scared that it barely moved. It squirmed and twitched a little, but had not attempted to escape from the box. An entire day passed with Nicky, and it all seemed so far, so good.

The first night, I left the box with Nicky inside in the small pantry-like room just off the kitchen. My father suggested I cut air holes in the lid and tape it closed to the top of the box.

I wanted to sleep next to the door in my sleeping bag, but Mom wouldn't allow it.

"He'll be okay," she said. "You'll see him in the morning."

I spent nearly the entire night staring at my bedroom ceiling.

Nicky was still in the box the next morning. He had barely moved from his position the night before. The food had not been touched.

"I should try to feed him," I said to my mother.

She immediately nixed that idea, sternly reminding me of what the vet had said about bites and rabies.

For several hours that morning, I sat on the house's side porch, the box in my lap, and watched Nicky. I saw the nose jiggle, the body shudder, the eyes dart. And again, there was no attempt to get out of the box, not one. I tried pushing the birdseed closer to Nicky's mouth, but he still ignored it. I put water in a bottle cap and placed it near him. Nothing.

"Let's put the lid on and let Nicky have some quiet time," Mom said.

We left the box on the porch in the shade.

Early that afternoon, I peeked inside just long enough to see Nicky move a bit. I thought I saw him breathe, and then I closed the lid. I did the same before dinner. No change. Nicky had scarcely moved. The water was still there. The food untouched. That night, we left the box on the porch instead of the pantry. Dad's idea. I pleaded with Mom to let me sleep outside in the summer air next to Nicky, but she thought it best that I stay inside.

"Nicky will be good out here," she said. "You know when you're sick and you just want to sleep? It's kind of like that."

Again, I stared at the bedroom ceiling. However, this time I eventually fell asleep, awakening later than usual the next morning. I could smell pancakes.

"Good morning," Mom said, smiling, as I walked into the kitchen.

I rubbed my eyes and adjusted my pajama bottoms. They had gone crooked in my sleep.

"Have you checked Nicky?" I asked.

My mother knelt in front of me and grabbed my hands.

"Honey, Nicky has gone back home."

I squinted the way one does when you're uncertain of what you've just heard.

"He must have felt well enough to go back with his family," Mom continued. "It's for the best."

I ran out to the porch. The box was tilted on its side, the lid next to it. The twigs and leaves scattered, and the birdseed spilled on the porch's concrete floor. I ran to the steps that led to the backyard and looked left and right. I hopped onto the sidewalk, wincing as my bare feet landed on tiny rocks, and ran to the middle of the yard. I peered into the trees. A robin frantically skipped from one branch to another. A rabbit scampered through the rose garden. I heard the distant bark of a dog.

The pancakes were buttermilk, smothered in butter and syrup. Mom put a little vanilla extract in the Aunt Jemima batter, something her mother had always done. There was a glass of whole milk on the table and some sliced cantaloupe in a small bowl. The faint chirp of the morning news came from the small speaker of the counter radio across the room near the sink, and as I snuggled into a kitchen chair, I felt the touch of my mother's hand on my head, her soft fingers delicately smoothing the hair from my forehead and away from my eyes. She took a seat at the table, sipped what remained of the coffee in her cup, and quietly watched as I slowly finished my pancakes in the low light of the morning, the sun filtered by the sheer curtains that hung over the kitchen window.

It was a big disappointment when Nicky left. And disappointment is a hard emotion to confront, especially for a young boy. But I had Mom. I had her delicate, careful understanding, her quiet wisdom. Certainly in the big picture of things, it was a dumb idea to try to make a wild animal a pet—and I only had it for three days, hardly enough to scar my psyche. But disappointment, in so many of its forms, would show itself again for many other reasons. And when the frustrations, disillusionments, and setbacks came for this little boy, my mother would be somewhere close.

Nazis in the Neighborhood

This story begins with Nazis.

There was a German family–first generation immigrants–who lived two doors up the street from my boyhood home. I won't use their real name, but the story was that Mr. and Mrs. Ackerman escaped their home somewhere near Berlin just before Hitler came to power. They were quiet, and kept to themselves in a small brick house in the neighborhood of steelworkers just outside Pittsburgh's city limits. They didn't speak the best English, which kept them isolated from many of the other households on our street. When the grownups would have a neighborhood picnic, no one invited them. When everyone else would get together for a card night, they wouldn't be there. You'd rarely see the Ackermans outside the house, except when she was sweeping the front porch, or when he was tending to his backyard vegetable garden.

To the kids in my neighborhood, the Ackermans were mysterious strangers. Kids talked a lot. The Ackermans were Germans; we knew that. But to us they were *real* Germans, and maybe even Nazis. It was unsubstantiated, of course. Ridiculous, really. But we were kids and dumb. All Germans were Nazis to us. Our depth of knowledge of the members of the Third Reich came from John Wayne movies and the old TV show *Combat*, so when we'd hear any of the parents bring up the word German and the Ackermans, well, it was easy for us to believe Nazis might be living right down the street. Why else would they hide from everyone? Why else would they not want to talk to anybody?

One morning I was walking to the school bus stop, carrying my trombone. I was in fifth grade and had just started playing. It was a cumbersome thing to lug around in its big brown, heavy case with its steel locking clasps. End to end, it was nearly as tall as me, but when I carried the case by the handle it looked a lot like a rifle case, reminding me of the violin cases that secretly carried machine guns in the old mobster movies. That's how I saw it sometimes and so did some of my school friends, who teased me about being some sort of outlaw or secret agent.

Mrs. Ackerman was out on her front porch as usual that morning, sweeping again. And when I walked by carting the trombone case, she appeared to shudder. Our eyes met for just a sliver of a second, and then she rushed inside her home, almost running, as if to protect herself. *She must think I have a weapon*, I thought, considering what my friends said about the case. *Maybe she was scared because of what she saw in Germany, all that Hitler stuff. She ran away because my trombone case reminded her of terrible, scary times in Germany.* Those were the thoughts of a little boy.

I asked my mother.

"Well, honey, they did come from a place that was very frightening," she said. "But I'm not really sure."

My mother's response confirmed nothing, but her ambiguity also did little to discourage my wild imagination. Maybe what my friends and I had assumed was right. Mr. and Mrs. Ackerman might be in America because they were running from the Nazis— or maybe they were *actual* Nazis and didn't want anyone to know. Maybe my "weapon" had them believing someone had found out who they really were—secret followers of Adolf Hitler, trying to vanish into the shadows of suburban America.

This preposterous story had been fueled by what my mother didn't say. And what else was I to believe? The Ackermans even looked like Nazis. She was always dressed in a dour old housecoat, her gray hair pulled tightly back into a bun, a stern and serious face. He was big, broad shoulders, shaved head. She looked mean; he looked evil. Mr. and Mrs. Ackerman had to be Nazis. No question about it.

And then there were the rumors about killing other people's pets.

A kid in the neighborhood told me that Mr. Ackerman hated animals, and particularly was angered when anything got into his vegetable garden to eat his lettuce, tomatoes, and carrots.

"He puts rat poison all around the garden," the kid said.

"I heard he waits in his bedroom window with a rifle, and when he sees a rabbit go near the garden, he shoots it," another kid said. "And if he sees someone's pet, he shoots that, too."

A neighbor's dog had been missing. Kids blamed Mr. Ackerman.

"He killed it. Skinned it. Put it in his basement," someone said.

That's what Nazis do.

David W. Berner

We had a cat named Zipper. It was a mutt. Stayed in the house a lot, but Zipper also spent some time outdoors. In the mid-1960s, it was not unusual to let your pet roam. No leash laws back then. My mother loved that cat. It had a mixture of shiny silver-gray, white, and black fur, and it would sit in your lap, purring for hours. While out on his night escapades, Zipper would snatch a mole or a field mouse, play with it, kill it, and then leave it on the front doorstep, a prize or gift. At first it was just an occasional thing. Then it started happening a few times a week. Soon it was every morning, on the door step another dead rodent.

One morning there was no mouse, no mole. And there was no Zipper. By afternoon, still no gift and no cat. That evening, Zipper returned without his kill and he was not right.

"Look at his eyes. He's sick or something," my mother said, her voice cracking. Zipper was listless, his tail pulled up and under his body. She picked him up and cradled him, petting the top of his head. Zipper did not purr. All night, he slept on the floor near the couch in the living room, refusing to eat or drink. And the next morning, he was still there. He had hardly moved.

That afternoon, Mom took Zipper to the vet. I went along. A few tests were done.

"I believe your cat has been poisoned," the vet said, directly and seriously.

Mom was silent.

"He appears to have ingested something. It might have been anti-freeze or rat poison."

"What do we do?" she asked.

The vet swallowed, looked away for a moment, and said, "I'm not sure there's much you can do but try to make him comfortable."

"How long?" Mom quietly asked.

"Could be a few days," he said.

The drive home was quiet. No radio, no talking. I sat in the backseat holding Zipper. I scratched under his chin, a previously perfect spot to illicit a purr, but Zipper made no sound.

For three days, Mom meticulously administered the medicine the vet suggested. It wasn't going to save Zipper, but it might ease the inevitable pain. Each day, Zipper faded a little further away, and finally on the morning of the fourth day, Zipper was dead, lifeless in his little cat bed, the one my mother had purchased in hopes it would make his last days a bit easier. My father buried Zipper near a tree in our backyard.

"Mr. Ackerman killed Zipper," my mother blurted after a somber dinner that evening. "I'm certain."

I was stunned. There was all this talk about how he hated animals, about the poison, the rifle, but that all came from my friends. This was coming from my mother.

My father was less certain.

"How do you know that for sure?" he asked, trying to divert anger. "The cat could have gotten into anything."

"He's a mean man," she said.

For several days my mother threatened to telephone the Ackermans and "give that awful man a piece of my mind."

Mom was not an irrational, accusatory person. She was fair, loving, and president of the PTA at my elementary school. She attended church each Sunday and had good words to say about people. She took my friends and me to the municipal pool in the summer. She always attended my little league games and my elementary school band concerts. She offered blueberry pies to the neighbors and kept a beautiful rose garden. And Mom didn't lie, didn't make crazy accusations. Plus, Nazis hate animals, right? *He did it*, I thought. *Mr. Ackerman killed Zipper.*

I told my friends; they told theirs. My mother conveyed the story to members of her card club over coffee and cake. Neighbors gossiped. Then, one late afternoon a few weeks after the outrage faded, the house telephone rang.

"Miziz Barner?" The voice on the other end of the phone was deep, but tentative, according to my mother.

"This is Gloria Berner, yes," she said, wiping her hands on her apron.

"Thiz iz Otto Ackerman."

My mother's face reddened.

"Id iz abowt yer cat," he said.

Mom paused, swallowed, sat down in a chair near the phone, and said sternly, "Yes. Go ahead."

"I amz zo zaury to hearz abowt yer pet."

"Yes, it's terrible." Mom tried to stay calm.

"And I wizh I cood zay I knewz vaht happinid."

Mom switched the phone to the other ear, fingers methodically tapping on the kitchen table.

"But youz zee," he said. "Dezpite vaht youz hear, I dooz nut putz poizin aroundz my gardin."

My mother returned the phone receiver to the first ear, and placed a palm on her cheek as if to steady herself.

"Peeple zays diz becuz two year ago I putz a homezmade repellzent out," he continued. "Mix pepper andz eggz and dizh zoap."

"I heard you put out rat poison," my mother said forcefully.

"Iz zo zaury abowt Zipper. Itz waz not me," he said softly. "Iz wood neverz do zutch a zing. Neverz." He said he'd heard what had been circulating in the neighborhood, and he was hurt, saddened. But he was afraid to say anything to anyone. "And my Engliz, it iz nut zo good."

The heat that had so quickly filled my mother's face appeared now to be slowly cooling.

"Well," Mom said, pausing to take a deep breath. "I guess I can understand."

"Tank you, Miziz Barner. I prayz for you."

They talked for several more minutes. I even saw Mom smile. She must have believed him, or at least was beginning to consider it. She had always been forgiving. I knew this about my mother. I was playing with matches once in the garage and almost burnt the place down, but when I told her I was sorry, and she saw that I meant it, she was quick to kiss me on the forehead. However, in the early stages of this heartbreak, Mom had done what so many of us do when tragedy strikes; she had hoped to defuse the immediate pain by blaming something or someone. The need to find answers to our sorrows is a common human condition. Sometimes, even the best of us miscalculate and allow our own pain to corrode our judgment, cloud our humanity.

"Did he confess?" I asked as Mom hung up the phone.

"He didn't do it," she sighed. "Mr. Ackerman did not kill Zipper."

"But he poisons animals, Mom! He's mean," I maintained. "And you said he did it. He's a Nazi."

Mom pulled me to her chest and held me.

"I think it best if we try to think differently about Mr. Ackerman," she said in a prayer's whisper.

"Then he's *not* a Nazi?" I asked.

"He's just German." Mom smiled and stood from her chair. "Like us, you know. We are part German. Your great grandfather was born there." Then, keeping an arm around my shoulder she asked, "What would you think of going to the animal shelter this afternoon to look for a new cat?"

The next time Mom saw Otto Ackerman working in his garden she smiled and waved, and he smiled and waved back. And now, as an adult, whenever I read a story about World War II, or watch a film that portrays Hitler and the Nazis, I consider Mr. Ackerman, how dangerous ignorance can be, and how the secrets people keep are rarely what they seem.

Piranha Envy

ow cool would it be to have a piranha? So cool. But that wasn't going to happen. So I got angelfish instead.

I tried to convince myself that angelfish were a pretty neat thing for a ten-year-old to have. They had that cool triangular shape and those long, elegant fins. But still, let's face it, they could never compare with a piranha. No possible way.

"Absolutely no man-eaters in the house," Mom said, dashing any possible hope.

I don't think she actually had her facts right on the man-eater stuff. Probably saw too many weird sea creatures in the Jacque Cousteau specials on TV, or some exaggerated movie about the deadly beasts in the jungle rivers of South America. Still, she was likely correct that a piranha could bite off the finger of its owner. The fish had nasty, sharp teeth and an insatiable appetite for meat. Plus, the fish clerk at the pet store said piranhas were illegal. I'm not sure that was completely true. But it was good enough ammunition for my mother.

"See. No one gets a piranha," she said.

I thought it would be amazing to watch them devour things. Still, we went with angelfish.

"These are best kept alone," the fish guy explained. "Angelfish do better with their own kind."

Seems angelfish aren't such angels. They can be aggressive, territorial.

We picked out a tank and a filter and three angelfish. The clerk put the trio in a plastic bag and filled it with filtered water from the store's big tank.

"They eat special food," the fish guy said, handing me a small tin of angelfish flakes. "This stuff is made of worms and larvae and insects. They're carnivorous."

"Like a piranha?" I asked excitedly. *Angelfish,* I thought, *must be the next best thing.*

"They don't have teeth or anything," he said, amused. "Not really."

"Will they eat other fish?" I asked, hoping to discover something scary or monstrous about my seemingly peaceful and graceful new pets.

"They can," he said. "There are certain kinds of angelfish in the Amazon and they'll eat brine shrimp."

The Amazon?

"You mean that river where piranhas live?" I asked.

He grinned. "Same place."

"So they're sort of like piranhas?"

The clerk laughed. My mother patted me on the shoulder. I eagerly anticipated an answer.

"Well, they are, aren't they?" I asked, impatiently.

The clerk paused, leaned toward me, and looked me in the eye. "If I were you," he whispered, "I would not put my toes in that tank."

I smiled. That was exactly what I wanted to hear.

Having a piranha would have made me the envy of my buddies. Maybe it's just the nature of boys, but I think all of us, especially when we're young, need to have a little danger in our lives. We need to push the envelope. We need to ride our bikes down a big hill without holding the handlebars; we need to climb high in a tree until the branches have thinned, and sway and bend from our weight. And when we are older and more careful as adults, wouldn't it be good to remember now and then to take a risk, even a mini one? You may not want to buy a piranha, but occasionally getting out of your comfort zone is a good thing. Try skiing when you've never been. Take a dance class if you've always considered trying the tango. Learn to ride a motorcycle. Skydive. Love even when you're uncertain it will be returned. Risking it reminds us that we are alive…makes us keenly aware of our pumping hearts.

I had the angelfish for a couple of years, and I still have all my fingers and toes. But who knows, maybe I'll head out to the pet shop one of these days and look for fish with very powerful jaws.

The Last Bite

Dogs have taken bites out of me. Twice. Different dogs. Different bites. Both happened when I was a paperboy. The first while collecting money on a Saturday morning, and the second while delivering newspapers on a weekday afternoon back when there were afternoon papers to deliver. One was a chomp on the hand, the other in the butt. There actually was a third time, but it wasn't the same thing. It was a far different kind of bite, one that has stayed with me much longer.

The first came as I reached my right hand through the narrow opening of a screen door. The homeowner was trying to hold back a growling albino German shepherd and hand me $1.25 at the same time. The dog, a muscular eighty pounds or so, must have perceived my hand as a threat. One of the dog's canine teeth put a hole in the middle of my palm. The owner gave me a rag, and I walked home with it pressed against my hand, trying to stop the bleeding. Next came a tetanus shot and a couple of stitches.

The next bite came in a sneak attack. A gnarly mutt of a dog came after me as I was delivering the *Pittsburgh Press* to one of my customers. I had folded the newspaper, tucking one end under the other to form a tight rectangle, and as I opened the screen door to place the paper between it and the storm door, the dog came flying around the north corner of the house, up the three steps to the small porch, and clamped its jaw on my ass. The teeth tore through my jeans, scratching enough of the skin to draw blood. Then the little coward barked once and ran away. I don't remember exactly, but I think I needed another tetanus shot, or some kind of shot. No stitches this time.

The paper route was a dangerous place. There could easily have been other dog-bite stories were it not for the quick action of owners who recognized the tenacity of their pets and corralled them before they struck—or my decision to refuse delivery until people secured their beasts. This was the early 1970s; there was no such thing as a municipal rule forcing dog owners to keep their pets fenced in. Pets roamed. Dogs followed you to the school bus stop or chased you as you rode your bike down the hilly streets. And because of this, bad things sometimes happened.

We got Sadie at the local animal shelter. She was the dog after my first pet, a full-bred collie. Sadie was part collie and something else, maybe Sheltie. She was sweet, loved to romp with the kids in the backyard while we played kick ball, and loved to follow me on the trails in the woods. I also remember her eyes. They were deep brown, like the dark chocolate of an Almond Joy. Because it was first time the family had chosen a dog from the shelter, I felt as if we had rescued Sadie from a terrible fate, which was likely true. Who would have taken her home if not us? I hated to think what might have happened if we had not walked her out of the shelter's metal cage that day. She seemed so happy, almost as happy as I was. She needed us. We were her saviors. We were supposed to take the best care of her that we possibly could.

For several months, all was well. Sadie got her updated shots, was eating well, had good energy, was friendly, and seemed well adjusted to her new home. And like all the dogs in the neighborhood, she was never restrained. She played with all the kids, other dogs, freely chased squirrels and cats. Sadie was permitted to be as free as she wanted. Leash laws came years later. I can't even remember if our town had a license requirement. It's hard to believe there were times like this, considering all the regulations on dogs and cats these days.

It was a summer afternoon, the screen door was up, and I was just inside the front entrance when I heard the unmistakable screech of car tires and then the awful sound of Sadie's yelp, a distinctive tight cry. When I looked outside, I could see a car in front of our house, its wheels turned awkwardly toward the curb, and Sadie trying to run but instead limping up the driveway, her tail between her legs, her ears pinned back. She began to whine, a soft, sad sound. My father immediately lifted Sadie in his arms and gingerly placed her in the rear seat of his Pontiac. My mother took the passenger seat while Dad started the car, and I climbed in the back to hold Sadie's head, petting her front paws, trying to soothe her. Dad quickly turned the car out of the driveway and raced up the hill, heading for the veterinary hospital a few miles away. Sadie gasped, excessive saliva gathered around her mouth. I gently hugged her head. She gasped again, this time more loudly, and then she snapped at me, her teeth clamping around my fingers. It was not a fierce bite. It was almost tender, a bite out of instinct fueled by pain. She wheezed, gasped one more time, and fell silent. We were only two blocks from the house when Sadie stopped breathing. I had to pry my fingers out of her mouth. There was a minor cut on the index finger of my left hand, a small scratch really, but there was also a bit of blood so Mom thought it best to pour peroxide over it and cover it with a Band-Aid.

The wound on my hand took a few days to heal. Another, more significant one needed far more time.

Sensing Avalanches

The St. Bernard is a lovable polar bear. It lumbers around in life, moving slowly enough to control its great body weight, like a sumo wrestler. It also slobbers a lot.

"Just like your grandfather," Aunt Jackie said. "Just like Daddy."

Aunt Jackie wasn't a believer in reincarnation. But my grandfather was. And Heidi had Aunt Jackie reconsidering the concept.

"Heidi just might be your grandfather. It absolutely could be true."

Minus the slobbering, I presumed.

Heidi was my aunt's dog. My aunt fell in love with the breed as a puppy. When a St. Bernard is a puppy, it is like a small, fluffy pillow. You can't help being smitten. It's when it gets big that a St. Bernard's owner starts to second-guess what he's brought into his home. The issue is all about size, not disposition.

My grandfather was a truck driver for Kroger, a grocery chain on the East Coast. He was a burly guy, a man's man. He hunted deer on the weekends in the Pennsylvania woods, drank beer from cans, played poker with his buddies. And he had an enormous heart that sometimes compelled him to push the limits of the rules. During WWII when butter was rationed, my grandfather would secretly slip out hundreds of sticks from his work truck and into his Jeep. He'd rush home and go door-to-door in the neighborhood, passing out the butter before it melted. From time to time, he did the same thing with sugar. Never got caught. He would also clean the snow off the neighbors' walkways without anyone ever knowing who did it, secretly mow lawns, and at least one time, I've been told, he fixed up an old used bicycle he found and gave it to a neighborhood kid whose father was overseas fighting somewhere in Europe.

But my grandfather wasn't a saint. He had a hard side and harbored demons.

When my mother was a girl, she would frequently bring home stray animals. "Can we keep him?" she'd ask. At first, my grandfather would attempt to explain to his daughter that the dog was likely someone's pet and that it was best they try to find the owner. But my mother kept up this Pied Piper practice, and soon my grandfather was demanding she leave the "damn strays alone." Still, Mom would bring them home again and again and again. My grandfather became increasingly impatient and eventually started chasing the dogs away before my mother could get them on the front porch. And then one day, she brought home a cat. My grandfather absolutely hated cats. He drowned it in the bathtub. Inexplicably, my mother tried to bring home another cat. My grandfather shot it dead with a deer rifle.

"Just look at Heidi's eyes," Aunt Jackie said. "Those sad, melancholy eyes are Daddy's."

I was just a kid then. I'd put my arms around Heidi's formidable neck and hold on tight, her sturdy body able to withstand a young boy's weight. And I'd press my nose against hers, my eyes locking on those round, deep-set browns. I didn't know my grandfather. I remember him only from photographs. He started drinking a lot more beer later in his life, a half case a night sometimes. Some in the family say he fell out of love with my grandmother and in love with another woman and couldn't reconcile his feelings. Some say it was simply a matter of genetics. Men before him were alcoholics. I was just two years old when he died of cirrhosis of the liver. But when I was a toddler and looked in Heidi's eyes, I wanted to believe I could see my grandfather, see the benevolence so many remembered, see his virtues.

The St. Bernard, as the story goes, was used to guard the grounds of the Hospice St. Bernard in Switzerland and to help find and save lost or injured travelers in the Alps. They are animals that instinctively want to help and comfort. Plus, the breed's keen sense of smell and ability to detect storms and avalanches is uncanny.

My grandfather may not have been able to sense his own impending avalanche, and Heidi may not have been his soul reincarnated, but to this day I like to believe through the innate kindness of that 150-pound dog, I got to know my grandfather's goodness, even if only for a short time.

You're Under Arrest

I had a few run-ins with the cops when I was a kid. It wasn't like I was a punk, just a teenager. One winter night, six or seven of us bombarded a car with snowballs, pummeled the thing, each one smashing against the car's windshield at the same exact moment as it drove down our street. We hid behind hedges and trees along the road, counted down out loud—three, two, one—and then leapt out to rifle our ammunition at the car. The driver slammed on his brakes, quickly pulled over, and jumped out yelling, "I'm gonna kill you kids!" He chased us through the alley to the street on the other side of the cemetery, screaming the entire time, "I'm callin' the cops on you little punks!" We darted behind the church, our hearts thumping, nervously laughing about it all. Then we heard police sirens.

"Shit, he did call the cops," one of us whispered.

We stayed behind the church for more than an hour, hoping the cops would forget about it all. But it turned too cold and we dared to head home. When we got to the street where all of us lived, a cop car roared out from the alley. Some of us ran; some of us tried to act cool and pretend we knew nothing, saw nothing. I was one of the ones who tried to fake it. Not sure why I didn't run. That was probably more my style. The policemen in the squad didn't buy our story that we were walking home from a friend's house and knew nothing about snowballs and some car, but they also didn't have any real evidence. Still, the cops were certain we were involved, and they acted tough and tried to intimidate us, calling us "juvenile delinquents" and threatening to "take us to jail." I was about thirteen years old. The whole encounter terrified me. Luckily, nothing else happened after that confrontation with the police. We didn't know the guy in the car and in the dark of that winter night, we were certain he never saw our faces. It was an innocent prank, but now that I'm an adult I realize how dangerous it could have been. All those snowballs might have blinded the driver, sent him crashing his car into a tree or the side of a house. Being an adult takes the fun out of things.

It was about a year later when my buddies and I—the same bunch that whipped those snowballs—set a bag of dog poop on fire on some guy's porch. It was the classic stunt: fill up a paper bag with dog shit, pour a little lighter fluid on it, put it at the front door, light the bag, ring the bell, and run like hell. The police came around on that one, too. But again, nothing happened.

It was stupid kid stuff. Boys were supposed to do things like that.

I didn't stay long in my life of crime. I was busy with sports and drama club at school, and I got a job. I was a paperboy, delivering the *Pittsburgh Press* every afternoon and early Sunday mornings. It was the same route my father had when he was a boy, and a big route it was. Every afternoon there were sixty papers to delivery and a hundred and ten on Sunday mornings. It kept me busy and out of trouble. But what I didn't expect was that while making those deliveries I would re-enter the life of crime, for at least one day, because of my dog.

We got Soupy at the animal shelter. My dad picked him out. Dad fell in love with him as soon as he saw him and I did, too. Soupy—the name the previous owner had already given him— was a shaggy mutt. He was about fifty pounds and a loveable mess, his longish fur matted in spots. Soupy looked a bit like the dog on the old TV show *My Three Sons*.

Each Sunday at six in the morning, Soupy joined me to deliver the newspapers. We moved together through the alleys and between the brick bungalows on my route. He followed pretty close and was a good companion on those quiet mornings, happy as ever to be outside. I loved having Soupy around. But that didn't mean everyone else did.

"You need to get that damn dog off my lawn. Now!"

Those words came from behind me as I crossed one yard to the next about half way through the route, a stack of thick newspapers under my arm. I turned to see a woman, maybe about fifty years old in a faded blue bathrobe, standing on the stoop to a small porch.

"Do you hear me?" she questioned furiously. "That dog should not be on my lawn!"

The harshness of her words cut through the stillness of the early morning.

"Excuse me?" I asked.

"That dog needs to keep off my property!"

"Come on, Soupy," I called, trying to summon my dog quietly.

"And if that dog goes to the bathroom here," she bellowed.

65

David W. Berner

"He hasn't," I interrupted, trying to stay calm and reasonably respectful.

"If I find anything in my yard," she blurted.

I turned to face the woman and interrupted again. "The dog didn't go anywhere." It was harder now to remain composed.

"The dog should not be out here! Do you understand me?"

The woman would not let up.

"Seriously, lady, the dog is doing nothing," I responded curtly.

The woman stepped from the porch and onto the sidewalk. "You better keep that dog under control! You hear me?"

My heart pounded.

"Do you hear me?" she asked again, her voice rising.

"Jesus Christ, lady," I snapped, taking a step toward her. "It's a stupid dog. Relax."

"Young man, you cannot talk to me like that."

I was sixteen years old. My hair was in the fashion of the day—long and parted in the middle. I wore Levis and a jean jacket with the Woodstock festival patch on the sleeve. I was sure this woman thought I was a juvenile delinquent, just like those cops did a few years earlier, this time a criminal with a dog for a sidekick, a hooligan with a wingman. Although the police likely were right at the time I was throwing those snowballs and setting that bag of poop on fire, I was certain this woman was out of line.

"You know, lady," I said, "people like you ought to be shot."

I turned and walked, Soupy stepping right beside me. The woman said nothing, although I heard a hard sigh, the kind one delivers out of disgust and shock. After about a half a block, I looked again for her. The woman was gone. *I told HER,* I thought. *Idiot woman,* I thought. *Took care of that,* I thought.

66

Soupy and I finished the paper route without incident, just like all the previous Sundays. But on the walk home up the street from the last customer's house, I saw a black-and-white police car parked in my parents' driveway.

Police cars and the officers in them, even now as an adult, ignite paranoia. It doesn't matter whether you are guilty of anything or not. Look in the rearview mirror at a stop light and see a cop car, your heart immediately beats to a quicker tempo. Drive down the highway and a state trooper pulls up along side you, your blood pressure spikes. You can be in the coffee shop, minding your own business, and two officers walk in—protective vests across their chests, handguns on their hips, big black boots—and you sit at attention. It could be the school principal walking down the hallway, the big boss unexpectedly hanging out in your department, the librarian shushing you…any kind of authority stirs unwarranted uneasiness. And for a sixteen-year-old, the anxiety is heightened. But despite my nervousness, I honestly did not immediately put two and two together. I did not believe the police were at my house because of anything I had done, and it certainly couldn't have had anything to do with the argument with the lady on my paper route.

I opened the front door. Soupy rushed in and nestled up against my father standing near the sofa, the dog doing his best to encourage a scratch under the chin. Uncharacteristically, my father ignored Soupy and turned toward me.

"Did you threaten some lady's life?" he demanded.

My mother sat on the sofa, her eyes on mine, as if trying to coax an immediate answer. And two police officers, both dressed in deep blue uniforms, sporting crew cuts and offering only stern faces, stood next to my father. The smaller officer held a spiral notebook and pen and continued to write. The other, a broad-shouldered man with a thick neck, gave me a silent accusatory stare, like the one the hard-ass football coach gives his quarterback after fumbling the ball at the goal line.

"What?" I asked, still unable to make the connection between this moment and the lady.

"We have a complaint," the bigger officer said. "A woman on Hazelhurst Drive is accusing you of threatening to shoot her."

"Oh for God's sake," I mumbled.

"Did you threaten to shoot this lady?" the officer asked.

My mother appeared worried. Dad remained calm, but his squinting eyes showed anger percolating just under the surface.

"She doesn't like my dog," I said, pointing to Soupy, now lying on his back, legs in the air, tongue hanging out. He was beat after the long morning.

"So you did threaten her?" the other officer questioned, looking up from his notebook.

"Do you own a gun, sir?" the bigger cop grilled my father.

"Well, yes. I have hunting rifles. I have a pistol upstairs under the bed."

"And you have registration documents, sir?" the smaller officer continued.

"Of course," my father answered.

"Do you use the guns, young man?" the big cop asked, his question more sharply delivered.

"Are you serious?" I blurted.

"David," my mother whispered, attempting to put a lid on my stirring annoyance. "He does not shoot guns, officer," my mother added. She knew I wasn't a gun fan, as unusual as that was for a Pennsylvania boy in a town surrounded by deer hunters.

"I fired a shotgun once when I was twelve. In the woods. My dad was with me. That's it." I shook my head in disbelief. "You really think I was going to shoot this lady?"

"That's what she claims," the smaller officer said bluntly. "Just answer the question: did you threaten to shoot her?"

My father's hands were now firmly on his hips. I didn't know if he was aggravated with the police or with me.

"David?" Dad asked firmly.

"Jesus Christ," I mumbled, a nervous smile slowly emerging. "This is ridiculous."

"You think this is funny, young man?" insisted the big cop.

"No. No," I answered quickly. "But it is a little stupid."

I detailed for the cops and my parents the entire story. I told them about my paper route, how Soupy was part of my Sunday routine, about Soupy walking on the lady's lawn, about the lady stomping out of her house and erupting in what I believed was unwarranted anger, about me trying to ignore it, and about ultimately not ignoring it.

"I told her people like her should be shot."

My father smiled. My mother sighed. The officer with the notebook lifted his eyes from his writing and looked directly at me. "You said what?" he asked.

"I said that people like her should be shot. But I wasn't going to shoot her. Jesus!"

The big officer looked down on the carpet at Soupy, a clearly relaxed dog, shaggy hair in his eyes, paws still in the air, tongue still hanging out, and said, "And this is the dog that caused all this?"

"That's the one," I said, bending down to scratch Soupy's belly.

"Not exactly a killer," my father smirked.

"And I'm not one either," I said. I wasn't trying to be difficult with the police, but in my own way, I was questioning authority here. I'm sure I'd done it before in some minor way with a teacher and my parents, but this may have been the first time I was truly aware of it. I wasn't about to admit to threatening this lady because I really didn't, and I wasn't going to let the police manipulate me into an admission, even some minor version of one. The woman's over-the-top reaction to me and my dog—that shaggy, hairy, goofy beast—simply goaded me.

The two officers looked at each other. The smaller one closed his notebook. The bigger one slowly eyed me up and down, and then sighed.

"Look," the officer said, "don't say things like that."

"I was frustrated," I said. "The worst thing the dog may have done is pee in her yard."

My father covered his mouth to hide an emerging smile.

"You have to be careful," my mother said, scolding me.

"I think we're done here," the big officer said. Then he knelt down next to Soupy and rubbed his head. "What kind of dog?" he asked.

"Just a mutt," I said.

"Looks like Tramp on *My Three Sons*," the smaller officer said.

"I have a black Labrador," the big officer said. "Five years old now. Sweetest thing."

Soupy rolled on his side and licked the officer's hand. "Don't be going after any old ladies, now," he said, addressing Soupy. "And you," he said sarcastically, looking directly at me, "don't be threatening to kill anyone or we'll have to come back. And another thing, try to keep the dog from urinating on people's property."

"I think I can do that," I said.

After the officers left, my father erupted. "Jesus, Mary, and Joseph," he cackled.

"Who is this lady?" my mother asked.

"Some sad, angry human," I answered. "And you know, she really probably should be shot."

We laughed. Even my mother chuckled. And Soupy? He really did appear to be snickering as he rolled over again on his back, jutted his paws toward the ceiling, and smiled a doggy smile.

Dad Wanted a Monkey

I had to put Bob, my golden retriever on a plane and send him to my parents.

"I just don't feel comfortable with him anymore," my wife said. I agreed, although in our hearts we knew Bob wasn't trying to hurt anyone. Bob was just being a dog.

Bob was a surprise gift from my wife before we were married. I always liked people names for dogs.

Here's what happened. Bob was about six years old. He was sleeping on the tile floor in the entranceway hall of our home. Our son, Casey, a toddler at the time, was crawling around and inadvertently yanked on Bob's tail. The dog was startled, and when he spun around and bounded to its feet, the dewclaw on his right paw caught Casey's face just below his left eye. It was bad, a sharp, knife-like cut. A hospital visit, bandages, and several stitches were enough to prompt a call to my parents five hundred miles away in Pennsylvania.

"Sure we'll take Bob," my father said. "It's too bad this all happened. Casey okay?"

"He's healing," I said. "It will be hard for us and for Casey to see Bob go. I know that," I added, confident of the decision but still sad about it.

David W. Berner

My parents, although getting up in years and less tolerant of added responsibilities, remained dog people and didn't mind the work that came with caring for them. They always had dogs in their homes from the time they were kids, and we had several when I was young. My mother fussed over each of them, mixing up special dinners of ground beef and sauces in a frying pan. And Dad loved taking them to the nearby woods, walking for hours, letting them romp and run. His heart soared when he could share his walks with a dog. At the time of the Bob incident, my parents had a small mixed breed with Yorkie or something in it. My mother adored the tiny thing. And although I knew Dad cared for it too, I was certain Bob would be more to my father's taste in canines. Mom loved dogs, but I think my father needed them, especially big dogs. They gave him permission to show emotion, manly affection, the kind that wasn't always easy for my father, a man who grew up in a family that praised stoicism.

But what Dad really wanted was a monkey.

"A chimp, I think. Or maybe one of those with the curly tail you see sitting on the shoulder of an organ grinder in the movies."

Most Christmases and nearly every birthday that I can remember, Dad would joke, "Once again, no one got me a monkey."

My sister and I would laugh. Mom would roll her eyes.

"Monkeys are like birds. They'll just go to the bathroom everywhere," Mom would say.

And we'd all laugh again.

"No birds. No monkeys," Mom insisted.

Of course no one ever believed Dad would really get a monkey or that Mom would ever allow it. Where do you get a monkey, anyway? I had heard of people having monkeys as pets, but didn't you need a permit or something? Wasn't there some law? A neighbor on my boyhood street had a wolf. Well, it was part wolf, we were told. Kept it in a pen in his backyard. It even howled at night. Not sure having a pet wolf was exactly legal either. There was also a rumor that another neighbor kept a fox in a cage in his basement. Never saw the fox, but the word was the guy found it while he was hunting, the animal apparently abandoned when it was a baby. It grew up to eat out of his hands, we heard. And of course, from time to time you'd read in the news about someone keeping a mountain lion in their home, or several boa constrictors. Someone in Arizona had a pet tiger.

Was it really that crazy for Dad to have wanted a monkey?

"We should find one for him," my sister said once. It was a month before Christmas.

"You're crazy," I said.

"There's got to be a way to get a monkey."

Like Mom, I rolled my eyes.

My sister investigated, asking questions at local pet stores and receiving some limited information. Apparently monkeys are expensive, $10,000 or more. And you can only get them through special channels, breeders and particular pet retailers. But you could find one if you really wanted, although they weren't necessarily recommended as pets. "Get a ferret," one pet store clerk suggested.

The birthdays and Christmases piled up, and there was never a monkey for Dad. Year after year, he joked about it, and we'd laugh, Mom would maintain it was still an outlandish idea and scold Dad for bringing it up yet again. One holiday, I wrapped up a small stuffed monkey, the kind you might see at an amusement park, and gave it to him as a gag gift. And when my wife and I left Pennsylvania to move to Chicago—one of the few times I saw my father cry—I remember joking with him about how maybe now was the time to get that monkey. I was out of the house, my sister was growing up, time to buy a chimp! He smiled at the idea, certain I wasn't serious and was only trying to lighten the goodbyes. And when my first son was born, I clowned around with Dad about how what I really wanted was a monkey. Any faint, ridiculous possibility that Dad would ever get a chimpanzee or capuchin monkey had dissolved many years before and had become a silly inside family joke, a fun and obligatory put-on.

To ship a dog on an airplane, you have to go through a special baggage process. In a far corner of terminal one at O'Hare airport is a conveyor belt. Next to it is a desk and a clerk. I had to purchase a special pass and claim ticket, and sign a waiver that clears the airline of any liability, any responsibility for the animal's well-being during travel. I kissed and hugged Bob, looked into his big brown eyes and told him I loved him, and then guided him inside the travel crate. I watched as he rode the conveyor and disappeared behind the small curtain. I drove back home in silence.

Hours later the phone rang.

"Bob is here," my mother said. "He looks good. He's happy. No problems at the airport. We've got him in the living room with us."

"Thank you," I said, still settling in on the reality that Bob would no longer be in our home. "Hug him for me, please."

"You bet," she said. "Hold on, your dad wants to talk."

I could hear the rustle of a phone as it was passed.

"Hey," Dad said. "All good here."

"Great. Thank you, again."

"Yeah, but one thing. And I'm a little troubled by this." Dad paused and added, "I thought you were sending me a monkey."

Bob lived out his life with my parents. My mother fed him homemade meals, including the occasional treat of breakfast pancakes, and Dad took him for long walks in the forest, trimmed his nails—especially those dewclaws—and bathed him every couple of weeks in the basement's stationary tub. Dad found a photo in a magazine of a golden retriever that was the spitting image of Bob, framed it, and hung it on the door to his workshop. And when my father watched television, Bob would rest on the floor with his head on Dad's feet.

The Rolling Stones, with help from a children's choir, sing a song about how we don't always get what we want, but sometimes what we get what we need. Well, I'd like to believe Bob and Dad both got exactly what was needed.

Burying Dogs

(Adapted from *Any Road Will Take You There*)

It was the morning that my girlfriend's dog was scheduled to die. Cancer had eaten away at his right rear leg and for nearly two weeks, the flat-coated retriever had been limping and wincing in pain, the medication no longer muting what appeared to be an intense and continuous throbbing. The veterinarian said it was a fast-moving disease and the only thing to do was to amputate. Still, that was no guarantee. The cancer would likely return somewhere else in the dog's body. So, the appointment for the injection was set for 9:40 that morning, routinely scheduled as if it were an appointment with your dentist.

I was three years divorced and it was nice to have found a girlfriend who loved dogs, as I did. She had two. Phoenix was the older. He was a big, lumbering animal with dark sad eyes and a love of water, and when he was at his best, during his daily walks, he would race through the manicured grass on the local golf course and dive into the pond on the 16th fairway. He'd swim in circles, dunk his head a few times, and would leave the water only after being coaxed out, shaking the droplets from the oil on his coat. This is how I would best remember Phoenix, what I would see in my mind's eye when I'd hear his name. In fact, when my girlfriend telephoned that morning to ask if I would mind waiting to come up to her home until after the appointment at the veterinarian to give her, her son, and her daughter some time to grieve alone, I pictured Phoenix standing on the edge of the pond, among the cattails, soaking wet, quivering with indecision, trying to choose between obeying the call of his master or giving in to the pure instinctive pleasure of one more swim.

The phone call about Phoenix came just as I was returning home that morning from walking one of my dogs, a six-year-old yellow Lab named Mike, short for Michelle. I filled the water bowl, patted her on the head, and turned toward my sixteen-year-old son who had slept through the night on the living room couch.

"Graham!" I said, raising my voice enough to awaken, but not enough to startle.

Graham was staying at my home while his mother was out of town. Since the divorce, we had had an amicable agreement about where Graham would stay when she traveled. He had fallen asleep on the sofa late the previous evening while watching *Rambo* on DVD. His body—broad shoulders and thick, muscular thighs—was taking up most of the cushion space, his skin seemingly melting into the leather like butter on warm toast.

"Whaaa," he mumbled, his voice saturated with sleep and muffled by the three pillows stuffed around his head.

"We're going to the DMV. Let's rock-n-roll." I had promised, if we had time that morning, I'd take him to get his driving permit.

"Cool," he said, rubbing his eyes and shifting from lying on his stomach to his back.

"But you got to get up now," I said, standing over him. I could be a bit of a drill sergeant when it was time to start the day. Graham, on the other hand, tended to crawl his way into the morning. I still don't know how he got up early for those late summer, sunrise football practices during his freshman year when he was still on the team. That was before the grades started to slip, the bad choice of friends, and the school suspension. He ended up at an alternative school for a year. No more football. But the grades improved, and he was scheduled to return to his old school's classrooms. He had made a lot of progress. I was proud of him.

"I'm up, I'm up," he said, peeling his body from the couch, running one hand through his shoulder length hair and the other against his belly.

"Let's get going," I said. "I want to head up north to be around after they put Phoenix down."

"Phoenix is dying today?" Graham asked, momentarily startled.

"Kind of strange to put it that way, but yes," I said, trying somehow to come to terms with how planned and programmed this all seemed.

"Wow," Graham said softly, stumbling into a half-hearted attempt to find his jeans and his shoes. Earlier in the week, I had told him what Phoenix's fate would likely be, but now that the actual day was here it had become surreal. "Wouldn't it be weird to know the day you were going to die?" Graham added.

"I don't think Phoenix knows," I answered.

"Yeah, but we know," Graham said, pulling a freshly washed tee shirt over his head. "I'm going to miss Phoenix. He was my buddy."

Graham dog-sat Phoenix a few times as a favor and had spent an afternoon or two with him over the last several months. "I just think he was a great guy," Graham said. "Kind of goofy, like a big oaf, but I loved him. I'm going to miss him."

"You really liked that dog, huh?" I asked sympathetically, a little surprised by Graham's reaction.

"He was the coolest. It's just sad," Graham said. "Where are they going to bury him?"

"Cremation," I said.

"Burn him? Really?"

"Yes, they want to spread the ashes, maybe in his favorite park."

Graham sat up on the couch, his usually active eyes quietly softening into a stare. Not one of blank thought, but one of singular focus.

"When you die, Dad, no one better burn you." Graham said.

"Why not, Graham?"

"I just don't like thinking about it. All that heat, the burning, the flames."

"I haven't really thought about this much, Graham," I said, grabbing my jacket and car keys from the coffee table.

"Seriously, Dad," Graham said, still sitting on the couch, his head now raised up, his neck stiffening, his shoulders back. "Don't do it, okay?" he said, his face now showing the clear signs of awakening and his eyes fixed directly onto mine. "Just don't."

I took a seat beside Graham on the couch and stroked my hand across the back of Mike's head. The dog had wiggled her body and her continuously wagging tail between the coffee table and the right arm of the sofa. Graham grabbed Mike just below her two ears, one hand on either side, and vigorously massaged her fur.

"Hey, girl," Graham said, lowering his head so he could have a straight-on look into the dog's espresso-brown eyes and shifting his vocal tone from serious to silly the way one does when talking to an infant. "Who's my best girl?"

I leaned into the back cushion of the couch and thought about how several years ago Graham wept at my father's funeral, struggled with the death of his cousin's drug overdose, and wondered aloud about his grandmother's failing health, her frequent doctor appointments and hospital stays. Graham wore his emotions like badges, shiny on his chest...his sorrows, worries, and joys served up like offerings to those willing to accept them without condition. And like an arm wrapping around the shoulders of a troubled friend, Mike put her nose on Graham's knee and let out a soft sigh.

Graham, like me, was a dog person. Part of that condition is hardwired, innate, and another part is pure experience. If you grow up with a dog, live with a dog, then almost through osmosis the dog becomes a vital ingredient of your existence. I had a dog in my life from the time I was a baby. And after thirteen years of companionship, on a humid and sunny Fourth of July, following several days of labored breathing and a complete loss of appetite, my first dog, a sweet collie named Sally, died of old age. My father cried as he dug her grave.

"Damn fireworks," he muttered as he stabbed his spade into the soft ground under the towering white pine in our front yard.

Sally hated the cracks and pops of firecrackers, cherry bombs, and M-80s. The explosive sounds pierced her ears and sent her scurrying from the noise to cower in a dark corner of our basement.

Sally was the first dog my parents buried in our yard. In the suburb of Pittsburgh where I grew up, it was illegal to bury anything on your property, but that didn't stop my family from putting all of our dogs, a total of six over time, in the ground on our quarter-acre lot. Two dogs were buried under a couple of old maples, another under a big rhododendron, one by the south fence lined with forsythia, and another next to Sally under the front yard pine tree. Each time a dog died, my father dug a hole, lined it with lime, placed or dragged the pet's body down into it, spread more lime, and completed the job with shovels of dirt.

"She hated that damn noise," my father said under his breath as he shoveled earth, soft clay, and small rocks at a quicker pace, his face flushing and the volume of his voice increasing with each toss. "She hates this. Jesus Christ, stop shooting off the goddamn firecrackers!"

I sat on the front porch steps as my father finished his job. I was stunned and a bit frightened by what had unfolded just a few feet before me. There were tears I hadn't seen before, angry words aimed toward God I hadn't heard my father say, and an anxiety I had not experienced. My father's steadfast calm had disappeared. Raw emotion, vulnerability, his own insecurities, all that he had stoically tried to mask in an attempt to secure his young son's emotional safety had evaporated.

The old memory of the day my father dug Sally's grave continues to surface at unexpected times, arises from the mind's attic in unexplained flashes, in photographic form, pictures from a camera. And when it does, I not only see my beloved dog, but I also see my father, the beads of sweat on his brow, tamping the final throws of earth on a mound under a soaring evergreen tree.

It's the kind of memory—the dead pet and a grieving family—that so often turns into the storyline of sentimentalized fiction, exploitable emotions used to pull the easily accessible string dangling from the heart. But, the experience is forever authentic, deeply human, and far more meaningful than what might be evoked in the pages of a sappy novel or a clichéd Hollywood tearjerker. The death of my dog, like the death of my father's stoicism, is woven into my life in complex herringbone patterns, the back-and-forth weave of a sturdy, reliable garment worn over and over.

I stood from the couch and slapped Graham on the back. "All right, let's do it. Let's get you legal and get that driving license."

"Let's drive!" Graham growled with enthusiasm, the way an athlete gets psyched-up with his teammates before a game.

I gave Mike a little scratch behind the right ear and moved from the couch toward the door. "You know, Graham. If you don't cremate me, you'll have to bury me. And maybe I should be buried in the backyard at your grandmother's with all the dogs."

"I don't think there's room," Graham said, laughing.

"Maybe you could bury me on top of one of them, or build a tomb, a mausoleum, or something. Dig up the dogs, put us all in there."

"Okay, you're getting goofy now, Dad."

"Come on. Who else would you want to spend eternity with than your most trusted friends ever?"

Graham knew I was being silly, trying to lighten up the mood of the morning. He looked at me, tilted his head, put a smirk on his face and his hands on his hips. "Dad. You are too freakin' weird."

"Seriously, you could put the names of each of us on the tomb. All of those dogs…and DAD!"

We laughed, forgetting for a moment what the day would eventually bring, the reality of a difficult goodbye. And Mike, sensing only the pleasure in the room the uncanny way dogs often do, quickly stood from her lying position and twisted her way in between us, her tail wagging her entire body, her ears slightly folding toward her back and her mouth open, allowing her thick, pink tongue to fall out from the side of her snout as if she too were laughing.

Lizard vs. Sloth

Sometimes you just don't know what the hell you're doing. I bought the kids a gecko. I didn't know anything about reptiles. My brother-in-law had a snake once, or maybe it was his roommate who had it, but either way it was a snake, a big one. Ate mice, if I remember correctly. I had a little turtle once for a few days, but that's about as reptilian as things got with me. Most boys go through a stage when they want some creepy, crawly, slimy thing for a pet. I never really had that phase. And I'm not sure what prompted the purchase of the gecko. It might have been a request from one of my two sons, or maybe the latent reptile-envy I had been denying since my boyhood days had finally emerged.

Like I said, sometimes you just don't know what they hell you're doing.

It wasn't anything special. Not some exotic gecko of some kind. It cost just a few bucks. In fact, I initially called it a gecko, but I'm not sure that's what it really was. I was told later it was more likely what is called an anole. It was a little longer than a man's hand, green, and had one of those throats that fans out. And it changed colors, like a chameleon. They weren't dramatic hues, but the changes were quite noticeable. It was cool, even if

I didn't know exactly what kind of reptile I was dealing with or what I was in for.

I bought a small glass tank aquarium. It was what the pet store clerk suggested.

"Throw some rocks and twigs in there," said the clerk, a teenage boy with shaggy hair and a wrinkled polo shirt with the pet shop's logo on the chest. "You can get some real plants if you want, but these fake ones are okay," he added, displaying the plastic version in his hands. He seemed to know what he was talking about.

"The lizard is not going to know the difference, anyway, right?" I suggested.

"It's for looks, so…" he said.

I also bought a small fluorescent lamp for the tank.

"Lizards like it a little hot," the clerk said.

The lamp would keep it between seventy-five and eighty degrees during the day. When you turned it off at night, things would cool down, just like a night in the desert.

"You might want to buy two lizards," he said.

"They get lonely?" I asked.

"Don't know for sure. But anoles live in colonies, so…"

I nixed that idea. I wasn't sure what I was doing with one, let alone two.

"What do they eat?" I asked.

"Crickets."

He showed me his supply. Big ones, little ones, cream-colored ones, black ones. Who knew there were so many kinds of crickets? "Best to keep them in a separate habitat," he said. "And gut-load them."

"Do what?" I asked.

"Feed the crickets good vegetation, plants and stuff. That way when the anole eats the cricket, he's also getting good nutrition, so…" he said.

Seriously? Now I have to take care of crickets, too?

"I think I'll wait on that," I said.

"You're going to want to feed the lizard every two to three days, so…"

"I don't want crickets in the house."

"Then you'll have to come back to the store and buy crickets every couple days, so…"

"Yeah, yeah, okay."

See, told you I didn't know what I was doing.

The boys and I set up the lizard's tank together. I had purchased a tiny bowl at the shop, filled it with water, and then placed it in the corner of the tank. It looked pretty cozy in there. Nice light. Nice rocks. Nice fake plants. It seemed a good home.

Over the next two days, the boys watched the anole change colors a few times, watched its throat bulge. And they gave it a name. I don't remember it though. Hank? Steve? It was something human-like, I think.

On the third day, I stopped again at the pet store.

"Got a lizard. Want to get some crickets."

It was a different clerk this time. He asked some question about the kind of lizard, the size. I gave him the best answers I had. Then he put six small, creamy-colored crickets in a white box that looked like something from a Chinese takeout place, and I headed home. We dropped one cricket in the tank and nothing happened. The anole did not move, no reaction, not even in the slightest way. The cricket crawled and hopped around a bit like it had no worries in the world. Then, without warning, the anole struck, snatching up the cricket in a flash. Swallowed. Gone.

We dropped in another.

Swallowed. Gone.

It was a little unnerving to watch, yet wildly entertaining.

In a few days, I came back with more. The anole ate up the crickets. All looked like it was going well. I told the boys they could do the feeding next time, and they did. And for a time, it was all rather engaging to witness. Then, the boys (and I) began to get bored. How many times can you observe a lizard eating crickets and still get the same thrill? I'm not proud of this, but we became complacent, and then we just simply were irresponsible. We neglected to fill up the little water bowl. The every third-day feedings became every fourth and fifth. The boys (and I) would forget to turn off the fluorescent light at night or back on in the morning. I was the adult. I should have been more conscientious. The boys were young; they were learning about pets and how to take care of things. I should have known better.

After missing yet another feeding day, I thought it might be a better plan to buy a bunch of crickets, maybe a dozen or so, and put all of them in the tank at once. Certainly the lizard was hungry after missing the regular feeding day, and this would be a more efficient way to nourish him. Plus, I wouldn't have to stand there anymore, putting one cricket in at a time. That had become tedious.

I dumped the crickets in and walked away.

This is what I learned several months later. The size of the cricket is important when feeding a lizard. Some breeds need smaller insects. Also, lizards don't eat in a hurry. They're methodical. They don't stuff their faces like humans do. So when you don't match the right sized crickets with the lizard, and drop a lot of insects into the tank with a single small reptile, the omnivorous crickets will chomp on whatever they can find, including your lizard. Yes, they'll start to actually eat the lizard. Crickets don't have teeth, but they have biting mouthparts, and if they can't find a suitable meal, they'll turn on the reptile to fill up their bellies. First, it's the tail, then the eyelids. Soon they'll go after the toes. And if you have enough crickets, and all of them are famished, every single one of them will attack your lizard and eat it alive.

I found the lizard stiff and lifeless in the corner of the tank. A part of its tail was missing; it appeared a piece of its foot was gone. It was no longer green but a brownish-gray. Two or three crickets sat on top of the dead lizard while the others crawled and hopped around, apparently satisfied with their meal.

I wrapped up the lizard's body in a plastic bag and threw it away, snatched up the crickets in a jar and let them loose in the backyard, tossed out the plastic plants and threw the rocks in the garden, and then cleaned out the tank with soap and water.

"Boys, the lizard appears to have died," I said. "I'm so sorry."

They were sad, but not devastated.

I didn't tell them what really happened. I was ashamed. I had let the crickets kill the lizard.

Weeks later, I finally confessed to the boys, and to this day I still feel creepy about it. Sure, it bothered me that I let it happen, but what disturbed me more was that I avoided telling the truth about it. We all make mistakes and justify human fallibility by dealing with the consequences of our errors. But the echoes of that mistake remain. And then there's the issue of neglect, that very human shortcoming that is rarely forgiven, a failing associated with sloth, that biblical word that ranges from letting the dishes pile up in the sink to disregarding the tears of your lover.

No wonder some people like animals better than they like people.

There's a Hamster in the Dashboard

Moe is dead!" he screamed. "Moe is dead!"

The announcement of Moe's demise rang through the house. There was no doubt about it. Moe's fat, dark brown body was lifeless. He was gone.

"No, no!" my son screamed again.

Graham loved Moe, our black bear hamster. Casey did too, but his death didn't exactly thrust my older son into bereavement mode.

"Yep," Casey said, peering into the cage and adding matter-of-factly, "He's dead."

The boys were eight and ten years old. A babysitter was home at the time of the discovery. Casey telephoned me. I didn't pick up. He left a message.

"Dad, we think Moe's dead," he said, feigning grief. I think he wanted to give the impression he was upset, to show respect, but the truth was he really wasn't all that upset. It wasn't that he didn't like Moe or wasn't a little sad, but in the big scheme of things, for Casey, it was something we should quickly acknowledge and get over.

Graham was different.

"Moe died. He's just lying there," Graham sniffled as I entered the house. "It's like his heart stopped and he just dropped."

Moe, who had grown to double the size of what a healthy hamster really should be, was lying in a heap on his running wheel. I put my arm around Graham.

"I think Moe simply got too old and fat. But he died doing what he loved, running on that wheel," I said, trying to assure Graham that Moe lived a good life.

"I'm sorry," the babysitter said, showing the boys, especially Graham, some support. "It's too bad."

I thanked her and walked her to the door. Casey followed behind. After wishing her goodbye, Casey said, "What are we going to do with him?"

"Well," I said, thinking through the possibilities for a few seconds, "let's give him a proper goodbye. Let's have a hamster funeral."

We'd put Moe in a small box, something left over from Christmas maybe, and find a place in the backyard for him. "Maybe we could say a few words about Moe, or talk about some of the best times with him," I said.

Moe was one of the boys' first real pets and their first experience with a pet's death. I wanted to do this right.

"He'd have a grave?" Graham asked.

"Yes."

"We could put some kind of marker on the ground?"

"Sure," I said.

"Who's digging the hole?" Casey asked.

"I'll dig it." It didn't seem right to let one of the boys dig the grave.

With a small garden shovel, I hoed through soft dirt in a part of the garden, about six inches deep. I lowered Moe's cardboard box into it and slowly, somberly pushed earth over the top.

"I really liked Moe," Graham said softly, his tears drying.

"He really got fat, though," Casey said. "Probably killed him."

Black bear hamsters are said to be ravenous eaters, that's why the clerk at the pet store told us to carefully regulate his food. I'm not sure we did very well with that. Either way, his size was alarming. He grew like an NFL offensive lineman does when his career and his regular workouts are behind him. Black bears are supposed to be non-nocturnal, too. But that wasn't really the case, evidenced by the running wheel's annoyingly rhythmic squeak at two o'clock in the morning.

"He had a good life," I assured the boys.

"Except for that one time when he almost died. You almost killed him." Casey said.

"I did?" I said, perplexed.

"We just got him. He escaped. Remember?" Casey asked, annoyed that I didn't recall the incident.

"Yeah, Dad," Graham said, as if putting an exclamation point on the story.

"How did I almost kill Moe?"

"He got loose in the car," Graham said, hoping to jog my memory with snippets of what happened. "He could have died."

It was just a few days after bringing Moe home from the pet store. The boys and I were running errands, and I suggested we bring Moe in the car with us for a ride to the hardware store.

I thought it would be fun. The boys agreed. We put him in a shoebox, threw some shredded newspaper at the bottom, cut a dime-sized hole in the side for air, and put the lid on tight.

"He'll be okay out here," I said to the boys after Graham asked me what we should do with him when we went inside the store.

"By himself?" Graham asked.

"Sure, we'll only be a few minutes."

"I don't know, Dad," Casey insisted.

We left the box on the front passenger seat and headed inside. I think I purchased paint and some brushes, and maybe some wood stain for a house project. If not, then probably some small wall anchors for hanging pictures. I don't remember. But I certainly recall what happened when we returned.

Casey climbed in the rear and Graham took the front seat again, placing Moe's box on his lap. Just before I turned the car's ignition, he looked inside.

"Moe's gone!"

"What?" I froze.

"Graham, what did you do?" Casey yelled angrily. He was quick to blame his brother.

"He's gone! He's not in the box!" Graham shrieked.

"Son of a bitch," I said under my breath, trying unsuccessfully to stay calm.

The small hole cut into the box's side had been chewed to the size of a half dollar and Moe had squeezed out.

"Start looking around the car," I barked. "Damn it." Any attempt at composure had vanished.

"I knew it," Casey said smugly.

"Just look for him," I said.

Graham climbed to the front floor and peered under the passenger seat. Casey did the same from the rear, looking under mine. I reached below the dashboard near the steering column and felt around. No Moe.

"He has to be here," I asserted. "The doors and windows were locked."

In the middle of the rear seat was a small storage cubicle covered by a plastic lid.

"Casey, check in there," I asked.

"How would he get in there?" Casey wondered aloud.

"Just look."

No Moe.

"Graham, open the glove compartment," I ordered.

"Seriously?" he asked.

"Hamsters are good squeezers," I said, exasperated. "He could be anywhere and if I start the car, well, Jesus, he could be in the engine area and he could be mangled or burst into flames or something." I didn't know why I had suddenly become so dramatic, creating ridiculous possibilities that did nothing but agitate and distress the boys. Not a good parental move.

"Don't start the car!" Graham grabbed my arm and shook it. "Don't start it!"

I reached over him and clicked open the glove compartment, thrust my hand inside, pushing papers and old Life Saver rolls and forgotten sunglasses out of the way.

No Moe.

"Shit," I whispered.

"Dad? Where is he?" Graham's eyes welled up.

"He got out," Casey said. "He had to. He's not here."

"We'll find him," I vowed, reaching both hands down in the crevice between the two front seats. "Don't worry. We'll find him."

Casey sighed and leaned hard against the rear seat. Graham crossed his arms tightly over his chest and rested his head against the passenger side window.

"He can't just disappear," I said, reaching again past the steering wheel and under the dash, this time on the passenger side. "And if he's in the engine, well I'll just look under the hood. He'll be okay. Moe's okay."

Just as I was opening the door and pulling the keys out from the ignition, I heard a rustle.

"Wait," I hushed. "Listen."

Another scratch.

"There!" Graham pointed to the center console, a part of the lower dashboard. Just in front of the gearshift was a rectangular storage area with a small door designed for CDs. "He's in there!"

I pressed the release button on the compartment and there, crammed inside was Moe, his twitching nose pointed in the air, his small black eyes seemingly searching for answers to the unexpected adventure.

"You are kidding me," I said, enunciating each word.

"Moe!" Graham screamed.

"How did he get in there?" Casey asked without expecting any answer.

Graham cradled his hands around Moe and wiggled him out of the dash's CD storage case. He pressed Moe's body against his cheek and asked, "Moe, what are you doing, buddy?"

"No worries about starting the car now," said Casey.

"Yeah, Dad," Graham scolded. "You could have killed him."

"I'm just glad we found him. He must have squeezed his way under the dashboard from behind and settled into the console," I said, trying to explain Moe's escapade. "And just for the record, I wasn't going to start the car, guys. Not until we found him."

"Good thing," Graham said, now clutching Moe to his chest.

"Do me a favor," I said to Graham. "Hold him in your hands, tight, until we get home and we can put him in the damn cage."

I smoothed over the dirt on Moe's grave and Graham placed a single marigold blossom he'd plucked from the pots on the deck on top of the small mound. We chose from the garden an interesting small stone, one with veins of color and tamped it into the soil as a sort of monument.

After a few moments I asked, "You guys like to say something?"

Casey, with his eyes on the grave, shook his head. Graham cleared his throat. "You were a pretty good guy, Moe," he said, "even though you tried to get away and you got fat."

There would be more pets and inevitably (and unfortunately) we'd have to endure their deaths. But there would be no other animal in the boys' lives that would be able to pull off a Houdini act like the one pulled off by big, old Moe.

Why I No Longer Like the Zoo

I could see something in the middle of the fairway about a hundred yards in front of me, a small black paper bag or maybe a rock. It was quite curious out there in the bright sun and green grass, out of place, odd. I walked closer.

I had slipped away for an afternoon of nine holes, carrying my bag. Beautiful day. Slight breeze. Not hot. The course had a stream that ran through it and pockets of wetlands, a nature oasis between suburban homes and apartment complexes.

Whatever it was in the fairway did not move. I squinted my eyes, hoping to identify it. Then, from about forty yards away, it seemed to shake, and then at the speed of dripping molasses, it began to move along the fairway.

I picked up my pace. It appeared to pick up its pace, too, although it wasn't much of a pace.

What was this? At twenty yards, I had my answer.

A turtle.

When I was about eight years old, my grandmother bought me a tiny turtle. It was one of those little ones that came with a clear plastic "habitat" with a place for water and a small island in it. I think she bought it at G.C. Murphy, one of the so-called five-and-dime stores around Pittsburgh in the 1960s that sold penny candy, laundry detergent, and men's underwear. In the rear of the store was a sad, rundown, in-store pet shop where they sold guppies, goldfish, and little reptiles. The turtle—no bigger than the palm of my hand—was a dark, odd shade of green. I have some vague recollection that the sale of those turtles was banned at some point in the late 70s. But when I had mine, they were quite popular, and I was simply fascinated. That was until I realized turtles didn't do much. Ben—the name I gave it—just sat there, sheltering itself under its hard outer layer. I would tap on the shell, hoping to coax out its snake-like head, but it rarely even peeped out for more than a second or two. The only time it was any fun was when I'd turn it upside down and balance it on its shell to watch it squirm and struggle to right itself. I think Ben only lived about a week or so. It was really a cruel thing. No wonder they were banned.

When I got a few feet away on the left side of the fairway, the turtle stopped moving and slunk inside its shell, clearly a protective maneuver. I picked it up by the hard edges and admired the bright orange and yellow markings, and then turned it over to see its brown underbelly. It was so tightly pulled into itself, it appeared as if it had no head or legs at all.

"What's up, little buddy?" I whispered to the turtle. "You are pretty darn neat."

Then, without much hesitation, I zipped open the long pocket that ran the length of my golf bag and gently put the turtle inside.

"Won't the boys find this cool," I said to myself.

I played four more holes with the turtle at the bottom of my bag, opening the pocket every few minutes to see if it was okay. It stayed curled up inside its shell and probably was in terrible anguish.

The boys weren't home from school when I arrived at the house. So I placed the turtle, still hiding under its shell, in the stationary tub in the laundry room and turned on the faucet to put a little water at the bottom, hoping this might give it a sense of well being. Silly thought, really, especially when all the turtle did once it sensed the unnatural hard plastic tub under its belly was scratch at the tub's bottom edges in a desperate attempt to escape.

I searched the Internet. Some website suggested it was a box turtle. It was about eight inches long and had the same markings on the shell as the one in the online photo. The site said it ate worms and insects and occasionally weeds. The box turtle rarely bit anything out of aggression, but would if provoked or threatened. I looked again into the tub. The turtle did not look happy.

I read some more.

Apparently the box turtle is common in North America. It largely restricts its activities to mornings and after rains. When it gets too hot, it nestles under decaying logs and mud. Males tend to have red eyes and females have yellowish ones. This one had red, so a boy. They don't necessarily mate for life, but some have been known to stay together with a partner for many years. Some can live to be fifty to sixty years old. When they mate, the male stands on its back legs to mount the female, and sometimes can get so rowdy in the act it topples over on his back, can't right itself, and dies of starvation. There's probably a joke in there somewhere.

But of all the things I read on the website about the box turtle, there was one thing that shook me up a bit. Box turtles are homebodies. Serious homebodies. They tend to live their entire lives in a space no bigger than 750 feet in diameter. All those many years, the turtle stays in a very small universe. It finds a home and it never leaves. I now felt absolutely awful. By putting the turtle in my golf bag and selfishly bringing it to the house for the boys to see, I had taken it away from its only home, away from its wife, kids, and the only world it had ever known.

I looked down into the stationary tub, observing anxious scratching and what appeared to be attempts at jumping.

"Dad!" Graham yelled. He was home from elementary school and saw my car in the driveway.

"In here," I yelled back. "I got something to show you."

"Look," I said, pointing to the tub.

Graham gasped then said, "Can I touch it?"

"Sure, but be careful. He doesn't look too happy."

I told Graham where it came from, how I got it home, and maybe it would be a good idea to find some worms to feed it.

"Are we going to keep it?" he asked. I wasn't sure if he was asking because he wanted to hear a yes or because he believed it was a crazy idea.

I thought about the little turtle I had as a kid, and about the habitat of the turtle now in front of me. I thought about the tiny range of its home. I thought about its long life and how old it might be. I thought about the other turtles on the golf course and in the nearby wetlands. I thought about its mate, its offspring.

The front door burst open again.

"Dad, are you here?" Casey asked.

"We're in the laundry room," Graham said. "Dad brought home a turtle."

Casey was in middle school and at that age when not much appeared to excite him, or at least not enough for him to show it.

He looked into the tub.

"Seriously?" he asked. "Why?"

I told him the story about the golf course, the strange object on the fairway. I told him about the life of a box turtle and the small place they called home.

"And you brought it to the house in your golf bag?" he questioned, as if calculating his father's mental state.

"I made sure he was okay," I said, attempting to assure him.

"We're not going to keep it?" Casey's question seemed accusatory.

"I just wanted you to see it." That was a lie. I had initially thought about them keeping it, and now was backpedaling. "Don't think you've ever seen a real turtle, a big one like this up close, right?"

The turtle continued to scratch at the tub's edges.

All three us stared in silence for several minutes.

That evening just before sunset, we put the turtle in a shoebox and drove the car to a spot behind a gas station where it was easy to access a calm and shallow section of the DuPage River. The golf course was closed and we couldn't get on the property, so the river seemed the next best thing. All three of us walked to the water's edge, I put the box on the ground, and lightly shook it to persuade the turtle to crawl out. It did and then scooted, as much as a turtle can scoot, down the small embankment and into the weedy vegetation.

I'm not sure what immediately compelled me to grab the turtle, stuff it in my golf bag, and bring it home. Maybe, in part, I did it for the same reason humans have zoos, the same reason that we go to them. And maybe there is some merit to that sort of regulated captivity—a primitive, imperfect way to experience the animals we may never be able to experience without caging them and putting them out for public viewing. I had been to my share of zoos as child and to several with my own children, and I do remember enjoying them most of the time. But I can say with great certainty that after that afternoon with the box turtle, I will never bring another wild animal home in my golf bag, and don't believe I'll ever go back to a zoo.

Mike

et's clear something up from the start. Mike is a girl.
The name is short for Michelle. It belonged to the hospice
nurse who cared for my father, a high school nickname, she
said, that just stuck.

Mike's name stuck, too, although it was never really going to
be anything else.

I always liked the idea of people names for pets. There was
Bob, the golden retriever, and I would love to name my next dog
Stan or Steve. The name Mike was chosen even before I picked
her out of the litter of yellow Labs at one of those modern-day
dog sellers that looks like an old-fashioned pet shop but feels like
the home of a breeder. I still don't know if they're good places for
pets, but I found Mike there, and that's a good thing.

Mike was one of three puppies in an open-top cage in the
middle of the showroom floor. The eyes did it. They had me
right away. "Hello Mike," I cooed, kneeling to her level, rubbing
her ears and belly. Yes, I was sure I wanted to call her Mike, but
to this day I'm not *exactly* certain why I was so set on the name.
It's clear it had something to do with honoring my father and all
the struggles he experienced when prostate cancer spread to his
bones and took him away. But I'm honestly not sure. Maybe it

was the simplicity of the name, the way it snapped off the tongue when I called it, or how it echoed in the neighborhood the time I shouted it one night into the streets, panicked that Mike was not coming back and I had lost her forever.

It was a steamy summer evening. The sun was disappearing just over the rooftops of the homes across the street, but the sun had left the arms of the plastic Adirondack chairs on the front porch and the small metal table between them warm to the touch. The last few days had been somewhat stormy, and now the dry evening had beckoned me outside despite the heat. Mike was by my side, as usual, resting on the porch floor, her head nestled between her outstretched front paws. I read *The New York Times* from my Kindle as the light of the day slowly faded into the glow of the neighborhood's dim street lamps. I don't remember the article or the subject, just that it was one of those longer pieces in the *Times'* Sunday Magazine section and it had every bit of my attention.

I never heard the familiar tick-tick of her paws' nails on the porch's wooden planks, or the quicker thump-thump of Labrador feet scampering down the front steps. Mike never barked, never whimpered, never made a sound. It was as if she were a canine spy, slipping past the border to take on a clandestine mission for the good of the dog world. She disappeared into the dark night like the Dark Knight himself.

"Jesus Christ, Mike," I snarled to myself, frustrated after realizing she was no longer at my feet.

Mike had wandered off before, but this disappearance was peculiar. There had been no other dogs or people who had crossed in front of the house, sometimes a magnet for her attention. And the stealth-like way she seemingly slithered off the porch was curious. Plus, when she had wandered before, Mike rarely went far. I'd find her in the yard just next door or near the garage cans in the alley behind the house.

"Mike!" I hollered from the porch's top step into the dark. "Mike!"

Mike had been showing signs of age. She tuckered out quickly when we'd go for our walk, and when I'd come home from work she didn't always immediately greet me at the door. Sometimes when I'd enter, I'd see her slowly stretching her way out of the dog bed, and then walk meekly to me, her tail wagging with less enthusiasm than a few years ago. Even more worrisome was all the water she had been drinking. I couldn't refill her bowl fast enough, so she was continually sneaking into the bathroom hoping to find the toilet seat up. Maybe it was diabetes, a friend suggested. I was reluctant to take her to the vet. I didn't want to know.

I walked to the sidewalk and called her name again. "Mike!" I whistled and waited. Looked to the north and south, and crossed the street to the church parking lot. "Mikkkeee!" I didn't see her, didn't hear her. I moved to the backyard. No Mike. The alley. No Mike.

Hogan, the dog I had before Mike, was named after the famous golfer Ben Hogan not the TV show *Hogan's Heroes*, as some people thought. Hogan used to run off constantly, far more than Mike, bolting through my legs and out the front door as if escaping from prison. And then, frustrating me further, he would elude me for hours. I might see him in a neighbor's yard, but when I'd close in on him, he'd dart off like he was playing some devilish version of tag. There were numerous times I found

109

Hogan blocks away, and too many times I had to rescue him from the city pound after someone had called animal control about an unleashed dog scooting crazily between houses and running out into the streets. There was the time following one of Hogan's jailbreaks, after driving around for hours with my young sons looking for him and finally capturing and securing him in my car, that this uncontrollable terrier leapt out of my younger son's arms, through the open rear window, and out on to a busy intersection. "Hogan jumped!" my son yelled. "He just jumped!" I didn't actually see him bound out of the car, but in my peripheral vision there was this blur of movement and then there he was, Hogan in midair. He was suspended in flight, graceful like a deer. He hit the concrete, front paws first, and began dodging dozens of vehicles in four lanes of traffic, happy as ever to be free again, ignorant to the peril. I pulled the car over and corralled him on the northwest corner near a strand of tall pine trees. He seemed utterly unfazed, even exhilarated by the experience. Hogan got sick later in his life and sadly we had to put him down. But he somehow survived every one of his daredevil adventures.

Mike didn't do anything like that. Thank goodness. But sometimes she was oblivious to danger albeit for a completely different reason. Hogan was fearless. Mike was just clueless. She would saunter into the middle of the street in front of the house as if in some sort of trance, her focus on the alluring aroma of an empty, wayward McDonald's bag. She never missed an opportunity for food, or the smell of the remnants. Remembering this kind of previous behavior did worry me a bit the night she was lost, especially in the dark.

"Mike!" I moved a block up the street past the dentist office and Montessori school. "You didn't see a yellow Lab roaming around here, did you?" I asked the man stepping out from the white brick apartment building.

"Nope, sorry."

"Mike!" I shouted, peeking now between the houses on the west side of the avenue. Nothing.

My very first dog, Sally, was a present from my grandfather on my first birthday. "A boy should have a dog," he told my mother. I grew up with Sally. She was glued to me and rarely left my side. Then there was Sadie, the one hit by the car. Soupy, my third dog, once stole a steak right off the top of a neighbor's charcoal grill. When I left for college, my mother had a series of small dogs—a Maltese, a Yorkie mix, and another that was some combination of small terriers. All of those dogs are buried in my parents' backyard. It was a very illegal practice. My parents didn't care. They loved their dogs. So did I.

The rear porch lamp of one of the nearby homes shed a sliver of light across a small asphalt parking lot near the north end of the alley behind my house, and for just a moment I thought I saw something move across it. "Mike," I called with anticipation and walked closer. The lamp's glow seemed to have illuminated what could have been the white fur on Mike's face, a color that had emerged with age. I moved quickly into the alley, whistled and called again, "Mike!" Then I saw a yellow dog. Between two cars in the parking stood a smallish golden retriever. It was still for a moment, stared at me, and then ducked around a big pickup truck. The owner emerged from the corner of the lot near the garage cans. "Come on, boy," he said. The dog scampered toward him and followed him to the back entrance of the nearby apartments. I walked between the cars, thinking maybe Mike had trailed the other dog. No Mike.

I don't live in the heart of Chicago, but the near west suburbs are just as congested. There's a fair amount of street traffic, a traffic light at the corner, a bus stop nearby. It's a lot of activity for a friendly and not-so-bright dog to navigate. It had been nearly a half-an-hour since realizing Mike had walked off, night had thrown itself over the neighborhood like a heavy blanket, and I didn't know where else to look.

I telephoned the police.

"What kind of dog is it?" the female officer asked.

"Yellow Lab. She goes by Mike."

"She?"

"Long story."

"Okay," she said. "And the phone number to call if someone finds her?"

If? My stomach was queasy.

I gave the officer the number and my address.

"She's really friendly," I said, worriedly. "She'll go with anyone who's nice to her, or has food."

"Okay."

"She's also not the brightest bulb."

"Someone will spot her," the officer said.

"It's getting late," I reminded her.

I sat on the top porch step with my cell phone in my lap and took a deep breath. Cars sped by. A group of young girls, patrons from the Mexican restaurant on the corner, walked past, laughing and holding white doggie bags. *These are the kinds of people and food Mike would find incredibly interesting,* I thought. I heard the bark of a dog from the cluster of houses across the street, but dismissed it. The pitch was too high, the voice of a little dog. Mike's bark was deeper; it resonated. I looked at my phone's screen, trying to will the ring of a dog rescuer. "Where is she?" I whispered to myself.

Mike was getting old. She had, at best, maybe a couple good years left. This was a recent reality that seemed, at one time, so far away, but now was directly in front of me; something I could reach out and touch, but didn't want to. Death is like that. It is always there somewhere, lurking. When it's the furthest thing from your mind, it suddenly appears. And somebody, something dear to you, is lost. My mother used to say that death was just a part of life. She was right, but that doesn't make it easier to face.

The night my father died I was sitting in the living room with my mother after arriving just two days before from my home in Chicago. We knew it wouldn't be long. Late one evening, my sister climbed the stairs to check on Dad after a long day of visiting caregivers, prescription painkillers, and watching his body slowly shutdown. She frantically called from the top step, and I rushed to the bedroom. After months of doctors' appointments, radiation therapy, and a weakening body, Dad finally had given up. Any color that had remained of my father's once ruddy complexion was now gone, hues of translucent gray had taken over. His eyes were lifeless; his cold body curled into a fetal position.

Earlier that night he had been just lucid enough to respond when I whispered, "I love you, Dad."

"I love you, Dave," he slurred in return.

Dad's hospice nurse, Michelle—the woman known as Mike—had been at my father's side earlier in the day as she had been for weeks, washing his body, monitoring his vitals, softly talking to him about the sunshine outside. She even prayed a little. Michelle was the first to telephone my mother that night after hearing the news. "I loved your husband," she said. "He made me smile."

I continued to sit on the porch and wait. A bus roared past the house, and then the phone vibrated in my lap.

"Hello," I answered anxiously.

"This is Officer Stevens."

"Yes?"

"Someone found your dog."

She offered a phone number, said Mike was in a neighbor's yard three blocks away, and she was getting water.

It was difficult to see the house numbers, so I pulled the car over, parked, and walked closer to the front doors.

"Are you looking for your dog?" a man asked as he appeared out of the shadows on the narrow walkway between two homes.

I looked past him and there was Mike, lapping up water from a large bowl placed on the tiny lawn near a small outside shed. "Mike!" I called, scolding her. "What are you doing, girl?"

Mike snapped her head in my direction, her ears perked up, and she ran toward me. I dropped to one knee and wrapped my arms around her shoulders as she collided into me. "Were you out for a bit of an adventure?" Her eyes met mine, her muscular tail slapping against my leg.

"She was on the patio at Café DeLuca. People were feeding her bread off their plates," the man said. The restaurant was several blocks west of my house on the busiest street in town. "She was also in the fountain."

"You're wet, girl!" I said. The fur around her face and belly was soaked. "The fountain across the street? The big one near the square?" I asked. I couldn't quite picture that, but I had no problem believing it. Labs like water. Mike was no different.

"Yeah. All four feet in, I'm told," he said, laughing. "She's a sweet dog."

"She's sweet with anyone who has food," I said, smiling. "Right, girl?" I patted her on the soft middle spot of her head. "I really appreciate you hanging on to her. The I.D. tag on her chain is so worn you probably couldn't read it."

He admitted he didn't even think to look. "We walked her here from near the restaurant and gave her some water. I had a small piece of a boneless chicken breast leftover from dinner. Hope you don't mind."

"A little treat, huh?" I asked Mike. "You may have never come home."

"No. I don't think so," the man said. "I saw how she ran to you."

I thanked the neighbor again, walked Mike to the car, and lifted her rear legs to help her to the back seat. She used to jump in the car all by herself. No more. Now she places her front paws on the seat and waits patiently until I hoist her butt up and in. Once settled in the seat, Mike licked my hand and face, her tongue coarse and sloppy wet.

"Seriously, Mike? The fountain?" I asked, her image now reflected in the rearview mirror. I could see part of Mike's face, her pink tongue hanging long out of the side of her mouth, her chocolate

David W. Berner

eyes smiling at mine like those of a happy drunkard. "The fountain? Really?" I asked again. I reached my hand back between the seats, grabbed her still wet fur just under the right ear and massaged as hard as I could. Mike offered a low moan of appreciation.

Dogs go missing all the time. But not my dog, and I'm not sure what I would've done if I'd lost Mike that night. Although we all lose in life sometime or somewhere, I wasn't ready for this one. I guess we're never really ready for loss. There's no good time. Loss often appears without warning, without preparation, and even when we believe we've adequately anticipated it—like I did with my dying father—it still stings and scars. And for all the days afterward, we struggle to soothe that never-healing pain by summoning the ghosts and memories that preceded the last goodbye. We talk about the good times, the beautiful moments. We laugh; we smile. We collect photographs and stare deep into them, believing we'll somehow resurrect those we miss if only for just a moment.

Mike is still here. Still moving a little slow. Still distracted by a hint of food. Still wandering off the porch from time to time, but not as far—not back to the restaurant on that busy street, although I don't know why not. People fed her some pretty good bread. And she still will forever remind me of Michelle, the hospice nurse. And, of course, I'll always think of my father.

Just the other night while walking alone to Café DeLuca for a late supper, I saw a homemade notice taped to a light pole on my street.

LOST DOG.
If found, please call
Answers to the name Maggie

116

There was a phone number, an email address, and a color photo on white printer paper of a medium-sized, long-haired black dog with an uneven white stripe down the length of its nose, one ear bent at the tip, and sad but welcoming eyes. I entered the number in my cellphone and took the long way to the restaurant, looking between the homes, down the walkways, thinking of Mike, and keeping a watchful eye for a dog named Maggie.

The Real Thing

eil Young has this great song. He has a lot of great songs, but there is this one where he sings about how relationships work, how love works, how the emotional compromise that comes with the truest of love is never really destroyed. When we are in love with someone, he professes, we keep what we give away.

This is especially true when you love a pet.

Our love, the human love, has its unavoidable faults, its baggage and hang-ups. But a pet's love never does. There's that verse in the Bible about how love is patient, kind, has no envy, does not boast, is not proud. It's a verse that's paraphrased often and offered in parables in many forms in many religions and spiritual efforts. There's even a Zen koan—*When You Love, Love Openly*—that essentially offers the same wisdom. I think this is what Neil is singing about, the truest of love. It's the love we all hope to experience, strive for, but many times find elusive. It's the love we all want, the kind of love our pets give us all the time.

That remarkable level of soul sharing, that extraordinary love, is precisely why I wanted my sons to someday have pets. Not a family pet, but their very own, so they might know a bond of love that is unique and hard to reproduce. But this is not to say I wanted them to have a pet right away or without understanding what it truly means to care for an animal, or how important the internal and personal negotiations are in the final decision to take on a pet.

"You're nuts," I said when Casey told me he was seriously considering a dog. "No. Not now," I advised. His plan was to get a dog after college graduation and take it with him to St. Louis on a five-month internship.

"But look how cute," he'd say, smiling and showing me a photo on a rescue website of a fluffy, cuddly, homeless dog.

Damn cute, I'd thought. *Damn crazy.*

Casey did a great deal of homework on breeds and shelters. He made calls, searched the Internet, talked to dog rescue organizations. And the entire time he was conducting this methodical due diligence, I continued to remind him what a pet would really mean to his lifestyle.

"You want to take a trip to go see your college buddies, you'll have to find somebody to watch the dog," I counseled. "Do you want to do that all the time? There is absolutely no spontaneity."

Despite this, I knew I was also talking to an adult. He was twenty-two. He was going to make his own decisions, his own mistakes.

One afternoon we drove from Chicago to Rockford to see a dog that was up for adoption. He asked me to come along. I wasn't sure at the time whether it was for support or just to confirm the decision he would eventually make.

"It's a mix. There's some Lab in there," one of the two caretakers said. The women acted as foster parents for rescue dogs, and this puppy was the last of the litter.

"I'm not sure," Casey whispered after pulling me aside. "I think I want to look around some more."

We left without a dog and Casey went back to his research.

Graham, my younger son, also wanted a dog.

"A French bulldog," Graham said. "And I'm going to call it Sanchez."

I laughed at the wacky blend of dog ethnicity, if there is such a thing.

"You do realize Sanchez is a Spanish name, right?" I asked.

"Exactly."

Graham always appreciated the absurd, the goofy, the odd possibility of artificial juxtaposition.

"They're kind of ugly, aren't they?" I asked.

"Exactly."

Graham loved cute, but he really loved ugly.

Graham was still living at home with his mother, working at a part-time job and going to school. But he had been attempting, with some minimal success, to convince his mother that a dog would be a good idea. There was still a lot of discussion to be had about what truly made sense, who would take on the ultimate responsibility for the dog's care, a decision on a breed, and whether a French dog should ever be named Sanchez.

"You're nuts," I said. "With your mother's travel for work and your job, school, and everything. Really? A dog?"

"I love dogs. You know that," Graham insisted. "I would be good with one."

I had little doubt Graham would be a super dog owner. And for that matter, I also had little doubt that Casey would be good with a dog. They both are caring guys. They had developed a solid, healthy respect and love for animals. Some of what I had experienced as a dog owner apparently rubbed off. Plus, they had some reasonably good training—despite some unfortunate mishaps—with a hamster and a lizard and eventually Hogan, the family wheaten terrier. But I also knew just loving a dog wasn't enough. Love *isn't* all you need. Sorry Lennon and McCartney. I believe there is far more to it.

There was this thing I'd say when I was younger, in my late twenties.

"The woman who buys me a great coffeemaker and a golden retriever is the one I'll marry."

I had read that David Letterman once had two dogs. One of them named Bob; the other was Stan. I really liked the name Bob. That's what I wanted to name the golden retriever, whoever would get it for me. And I was, and still am, a coffee fanatic. So that combination, I joked, would really seal the marital deal and capture my dog-loving, over-caffeinated heart.

One afternoon, the woman I loved and hoped would someday be my wife came to visit for the weekend. Marie was living in Cleveland, and I was in Pittsburgh. In the back seat of her car parked along the curb in the front of my townhouse were two things: a brand new Mr. Coffee automatic coffeemaker and a puppy, a golden retriever curled up in a soft blanket in a box. It was one of the sweetest surprises of my life.

We married in a Catholic cathedral on a beautiful late summer day.

Honestly, I wasn't really ready for the dog. If you listen to what the veterinarians and those at the pet adoption centers say, we're supposed to be honest and truly consider our lifestyles and available time before taking on the obligation of a pet. I was living alone, working long days, frequently traveling to Cleveland and back. A dog made little practical sense. This is how I see it now, in retrospect. Of course, I didn't see that then. In fact none of this entered my mind. That puppy was pure love, and that's all I saw. Nothing else mattered. To consider the business-like pros and cons, the everyday logistics of conscientious dog ownership was beside the point. It wasn't even a little part of the point. It was not the point at all.

Caring for animals—the ones we've had, have, and those that'll eventually enter our lives—involves enormous leaps of faith. But here's the thing: animals take their own leaps of faith in agreeing to be our pets. Sure, animals, and yes humans, face life risks all the time in the effort to survive. We face danger from predators and the environment and disease. But a pet's leap for love is a longer, more daring one over a deeper cavern. It's innately unconditional, and ultimately more amazing because it endures like no other.

Here's a story of a pot-bellied pig. I read several accounts of this in local newspapers and online. I won't use the owner's real name here or the real town, but I believe this story will help you see what I mean.

The pet's owner—an older woman—collapses in her home. It's a heart attack. Somehow sensing the critical moment, Lulu, the family's pot-bellied pig, rushes out of the house and into the middle of the street. She stands still near the centerline, stopping traffic. Then she runs to her house and back out again into the road. She does this over and over. Finally, one driver stops, pulls to the curb, and follows the pig to the home. He finds the woman on the floor. An ambulance is called and the woman later recovers.

Now I know you can call this something other than love. Maybe instinct or animal intuition, but why *not* call it love? Why not?

Another story.

A farmer is working alone just outside his barn. He's balancing precariously on a ladder and accidentally falls, landing in a compost pit. He shatters his hip. He tries to call out for help, but the farm is remote and no one can hear him. For five days, his pet goat, Mandy, nestled next to him. She kept him warm through cold and stormy nights, never leaving his side.

There's the story of the two guide dogs that led their blind owners down more than seventy floors of the World Trade Center on 9-11. And there's the one about the cougar that attacked an eleven-year-old boy in British Columbia while he was walking in the woods with his young golden retriever. The dog bounded at the cougar, fighting it off, and saving the boy. I can go on and on, and I'm sure you've heard or experienced similar stories.

So, what do you think? Is this love we give our pets real love? And do pets really love back? Before you answer, here's some hard science to further my theory.

Researchers at Emory University in Atlanta have discovered that dogs have a part of their brains that is similar to the human brain, the part associated with positive emotions. I won't go into all the details of how the study was conducted, but the conclusion is remarkable. Scientists claim dogs indeed have the human-like emotions associated with friendship, caring, even love. It's not some instinctive plea for a walk, a chew toy, or a bone. It's the real thing. It's a fact. Right there in the science. And maybe other animals have the same capacity, the ability to experience honest-to-goodness love.

Casey finally got his dog the summer before his internship…a loveable, loyal Labrador-Australian shepherd mix. He named him Cody, took him with him to St. Louis, and eventually to a new home in Seattle. He takes it to the vet regularly, walks him, gives him flea prevention medication, and encourages him to sleep in his bed. Graham continued to negotiate with his mother for his French bulldog, but eventually found an insanely cute miniature poodle-golden retriever mix and named it Franco, a nod to the Steelers' Hall of Fame running back, Franco Harris. He cuddles him close to his chest and takes photos with him several times a day, sending them off to me in text messages. And Bob, my surprise golden retriever, may have been the best pet I ever had.

About the Author

avid W. Berner is an award-winning author, journalist, and broadcaster. His first book, *Accidental Lessons*, was awarded the 2011 Royal Dragonfly Grand Prize for Literature. David's second memoir, *Any Road Will Take You There*, won the 2013 Book of the Year Award from the Chicago Writer's Association for nontraditional nonfiction. His broadcast reporting and documentary work have been heard on CBS Radio and on public radio stations across America. David also teaches at Columbia College Chicago.

www.ingramcontent.com/pod-product-compliance
Lightning Source LLC
Chambersburg PA
CBHW060326050426
42449CB00011B/2674